TOFU
&
SOYFOODS
COOKERY

Peter Golbitz

Book Publishing Company
Summertown, Tennessee

Cover design: Jeffrey Clark
Cover photo courtesy of Protein Technologies International, Inc.
Interior design: Sarah Jean Schweitzer and Michael Cook
Back cover photo: Warren Hill

Some of the soy isolate recipes appearing in this book are courtesy of Dr. Barbara Klein,
        University of Illinois at Champaign-Urbana
Some of the green soybean recipes appearing in this book are courtesy of SunRich, Inc.

photos on pages 6-7 courtesy of The American Soybean Association
photo on page 15 by Peter Golbitz

Printed in the United States by
        Book Publishing Company
        P.O. Box 99
        Summertown, TN 38483
        1-888-260-8458

01 00 99 98   5 4 3 2

ISBN 1-57067-050-1

Golbitz, Peter, 1952-
        Tofu & soyfoods cookery / Peter Golbitz.
                p.   cm.
        Includes index.
        ISBN 1-57067-050-1 (alk. paper)
1. Cookery (Soybeans) 2. Cookery (Tofu) 3. Soyfoods. 4. Tofu.
        I. Title.
        TX803.S6G65 1998
        641.6'5655--dc21   98-11902
                                                CIP

Calculations for the nutritional analyses in this book are based on the average number of servings listed with the recipes and the average amount of an ingredient if a range is called for. Calculations are rounded up to the nearest gram. If two options for an ingredient are listed, the first one is used. Not included are fat used for frying, unless the amount is specified in the recipe, optional ingredients, or serving suggestions.

Table of Contents

Preface

It has been twenty years since I was first introduced to tofu and the wonders of soyfoods. And although it hasn't quite seemed that long, it has been a wonderful journey from a simple tofu-maker to a soybean information expert. The latter career is much more appropriate for my family and me, as we decided long ago to live our lives on a beautiful island on the coast of Maine—a location much more fitting to the work we do today.

Over the years, I have made many friends in the soyfoods industry and have been continually inspired by their dedication and creative entrepreneurship. It is to these wonderful folks that I dedicate this book. In particular, though, I would like to thank my wife, Sharyn Kingma, for her working with me side by side in the tofu shop and in those first struggling years of our next business, Soyatech, Inc.

Thank you to Bob and Cynthia Holzapfel at Book Publishing for their patience and gentle prodding; to Mark and Ginny Messina for their dedication to vegetarianism, soyfoods, and health; to the great people at Soyatech, Inc.: Keri Hayes, Joy Froding, and Linda Mansfield; and to the following people I have met on this journey along the way: Yvonne Lo, John Paino, Tim Redmond, Rich Eluk, Ed Pedrick, Larry Clofine, Dr. Lester Wilson, Dr. Wilmot Wijeratne, Steve Demos, Myron Cooper, Gordon Bennett, Bill Shurtleff, Bob Bergwall, Judy Brown, Tom Timmins, Paul Lang and his family, Raj Gupta, Frank Daller, Dan Burke, Elmer Schettler, Dennis Strayer, Art Mio, Dr. Edmund Lusas, Dr. Les Watkins, Wally Rogers, Rick McKelvey, Dr. Susan Potter, Harry Tanikawa, Steve McNamara, Michael Cohen, Michelle Smith, Jack Painter, Gil Griffis, Marianne Gibson, Roger Leysen, Anders Lindner, Gil Harrison, Dwayne Andreas, Jeremiah Ridenour, Dr. Ken Shwedel, Vicky Braverman, Adela Perez, Susana Dehesa, Carlos Anzueto, Allan Routh, John Robbins, Dr. Barbara Klein, Nancy Chapman, Becky Stephens, the Soyfoods Association of North America, and to the American Soybean Association and the 400,000 soybean farmers in the United States.

The History of Soyfoods

To many people, soyfoods appear to be a recent addition to the world's dinner table—a new group of foods perfectly tailored to meet the needs of today's health-conscious consumers. But in reality, soyfoods have a long and illustrious history, dating back over two thousand years to when the Chinese first discovered wild soybeans. Not only did they learn how to cultivate them and make simple and nutritious foods with them, the Chinese were also the first to realize the soybean's medicinal properties. Soyfoods were found to be helpful in treating various diseases, skin ailments, and other conditions.

The use of the soybean spread throughout the Asian continent almost a thousand years ago, as people in each region or country developed their own unique soyfood products based on tradition, climate, and local taste preferences. When European missionaries and traders traveled to Asia during the 1600s and 1700s, they wrote in their journals about being served tofu and soymilk and what the traditional uses of these foods were in everyday life.

The migration of Asians to Europe and North America during the 1800s led to the introduction of soybeans to Westerners. A number of Chinese tofu and soymilk shops were established in cities with large Asian populations in Europe, as well as on both the east and west coasts of the United States.

As broader interest developed in soyfoods during the 1920s, the first non-Asian tofu companies were established by Seventh-Day Adventist groups in Tennessee and California.

During that time soy flour began to be widely used in both Europe and the U.S. to make low-cost, high-protein meat substitutes. During both World Wars, large amounts of soy flour were used to supplement meat shortages.

Large-scale soybean farming and processing began in the U.S. during the 1940s and 1950s, spurred on by a rapid increase in demand for both protein meal and oil. During the 1960s, the United States became a world soybean superpower and began exporting large quantities of soybeans and soybean meal and oil to Europe and Asia. The amount of soybeans grown in this country increased nearly 500 fold from 1940 to 1979, from 4.9 million bushels to 2.3 billion bushels.

During the 1970s and 1980s, U.S. farmers weren't the only ones cultivating a growing soybean industry. As demand for protein meal and vegetable oil grew around the world, farmers in other countries also began to plant soybeans. Brazil, Argentina, and India have now all become major soybean producing nations, and China, where the soybean originated, is still a major producer.

1997 World Soybean Production in Million Metric Tons

United States	74.08
Brazil	28.00
Argentina	14.20
China	13.50
India	5.00
Paraguay	2.70
European Union	1.44
All Other	8.32
WORLD TOTAL	147.24

Potentially, there are enough soybeans grown today to feed everyone on the planet. In 1997, the world produced a record crop of 147 million metric tons of soybeans, enough to  supply each of the world's 5.9 billion people with 55 pounds of soybeans a year. This would be equivalent to 27 grams of high-quality protein each per day, more than one-half of the U.S. government's recommended daily intake of 50 grams of protein per person per day for adults and children over 4 years of age.

Unfortunately, though, with today's emphasis on eating meat and other animal products, the world's soybean crop is not used that efficiently. Due to the soybean's abundance, relative low cost, and high protein and oil content, approximately 85 percent of the world's crop is crushed into soybean meal and oil each year. The primary use of soybean meal is for animal feed, and only 2 to 3 percent of this meal ends up as soy flour or other soy protein products for human consumption. Soybean oil, the leading vegetable oil used in the world today, ends up as cooking and salad oil or as margarine and shortening. Five percent of soybeans harvested is used as whole bean feed for farm animals and for seeds for next year's crop. Only around 10 percent of the soybean crop is used as the main ingredient in soyfoods, and of that portion, an estimated 90 percent of that use is in Asia. That means that only about 1 percent of the soybean crop each year ends up as soyfoods in Western nations.

The Modern Soyfoods Industry

In the 1920s early proponents of vegetarian diets, like Dr. John Harvey Kellogg of Battle Creek, Michigan, became interested in the healthful properties of soybeans. In addition to studying the usefulness of soybeans in the diets of people with diabetes, he also developed and marketed North America's first meat and dairy substitutes (also known as "analogs") made from soybeans. During those early years, soyfoods were promoted primarily among the largely vegetarian Seventh-Day Adventist church and to other special interest groups.

Soy flour became an important component in food production during war time to make up for meat shortages which developed from the increased needs of the army and the disruption of farm commerce during war years. Unfortunately though, soy flour and soy protein processing were not well-developed sciences at that time, and as a result, most of the products were not that tasty. They were tolerated at best, but not widely appreciated. In addition, soybean-based foods developed a poor image and were seen as being inferior substitutes and extenders for more desirable foods—something to be used in time of crisis and shortage, rather than delicious, nutritious alternatives to meat and dairy foods that could be used every day.

During this period, industrialist Henry Ford developed a number of plastic and fiber products from soybeans and actually had a car built largely using a plastic derived from soybeans. Ford's dream of a mass-produced soybean car never materialized, but his work (and the famous photograph of him swinging an axe against his soymobile to show how dent-proof it was) continues to inspire those looking

for new industrial applications of this miracle crop. In fact, today research continues on new industrial applications for soy protein and oil in plastic, adhesive, and paint products, and a special fleet of public buses in St. Louis is now run on a soy-based diesel fuel.

In the 1950s and 60s, and during the meat shortages of the 70s, a number of food companies and meat processors used soy flour and proteins to extend certain meat products. These products were not popular with consumers who complained of poor flavor and color. As a result, many food processors felt the need to reassure consumers that their products contained "no fillers" or "cereal additives."

It was during the late 1970s that soyfoods began to gain popularity. In both the United States and Europe, new concepts such as going back to the land, living in peace, vegetarianism, and a more equitable distribution of food resources caught the imagination of an entire generation. A growing number of people began

to question the ethics of a meat-centered diet. In the book *Diet for a Small Planet*, Frances Moore Lappe wrote of the misallocation of food resources and the value of the soybean, and in *The Book of Tofu*, by William Shurtleff and Akiko Aoyagi, the beauty and tradition of soyfoods were eloquently described and illustrated.

The rediscovery of the soybean's value to the modern world helped to inspire a new soy-foods movement in both the U.S. and Europe. According to statistics gathered by Soyatech, Inc., over 2,000 new soyfood products were introduced during the 1980s in the United States alone, mostly by small soyfood companies. Products such as tofu, tempeh, miso, tofu hot dogs, veggie burgers, tofu ice cream, soymilk, and dairy alternatives all have become common fixtures in natural food stores and have quickly crossed over into main-stream supermarkets.

The pace of innovation and acceptance of soyfoods has accelerated over the past few years as news of these products' health benefits becomes more widely known and they become more available. Large food processors such as Archer Daniels Midland and Pillsbury are now teaming up to produce and market new soy-based meat alternatives. Tofu and soymilk sales are booming as aging American consumers begin to make the connection between their diet and health.

Recently published papers, articles, and on-going studies report that soyfoods are not only nutritious, but that they may also be capable of preventing and treating many of the world's deadliest and most debilitating chronic diseases.

A Closer Look at Soybeans

The nutritional content of soybeans varies widely according to the specific variety and growing conditions, but typically they contain 35 to 40 percent protein, 15 to 20 percent fat, 30 percent carbohydrates, 5 percent crude fiber from the hulls, and 5 percent minerals and ash.

Protein: The protein in soybeans contains all of the essential amino acids necessary to sustain health at all stages of development. But until just recently, researchers believed that soy protein was lower in quality than many animal proteins. These assumptions were based upon an old method for evaluating protein quality, the protein efficiency ratio (PER), which is based on the growth rates of rats as measured in laboratory tests. Unfortunately, rats have a requirement for one of the essential amino acids (methionine) that is 50 percent higher than for humans, making this particular method inaccurate when evaluating soy protein quality for human consumption.

In order to make up for the shortcomings of the PER evaluations, the World Health Organization of the United Nations and the U.S. Food and Drug Administration have adopted a new method for evaluating protein quality called the protein digestibility corrected amino acid score (PDCAAS). This method uses a comparison between the structure of amino acids in a protein and human amino acid requirements (called an amino acid score), plus a factor for digestibility, to arrive at a value for the protein's quality. Using the new PDCAAS method, soy protein products generally receive scores of between 0.95 and 1.00, the highest value possible.

Fats: Soybeans, in comparison to other beans, grains, and cereals, contain a high amount of fat. But as we have come to learn, not all fats are created equal. While some fats are considered essential for proper health, others are decidedly dangerous to consume. Many of our major health problems today are due not only to the fact that people eat too much fat, but also that the quality and type of fat being consumed is unhealthful. Fortunately, the fat found naturally in soybeans and most traditionally processed soyfoods, such as tofu, soymilk, tempeh, full-fat soy flour, and liquid soybean oil can be categorized as health-promoting.

Approximately 50 percent of the fat in soybeans is linoleic acid, a polyunsaturated fat and an essential nutrient that the body cannot create from other nutrients. Soybean oil can also contain as much as 8 percent linolenic acid, an omega-3 fatty acid which is believed to be beneficial in lowering the risk of heart disease.

Carbohydrates and Fiber: Some of the sugars contained in soybeans are not digested or used as nutrients directly by the body, but are digested by special bacteria in the lower intestine. As the intestinal flora in the digestive tract break down these sugars, they can create flatulence. Even so, these sugars are considered healthful by some people and are now being marketed by Japanese companies as a health food supplement and food ingredient.

The insoluble carbohydrates in soybeans (cellulose, hemi-cellulose, and pectins) are considered to be the dietary fiber of the soybean. This fiber helps the body keep cholesterol levels low, maintains proper elimination, and protects against colon cancer and other chronic diseases of the digestive system.

Vitamins and Minerals: In addition to providing high-quality protein, fats, and carbohydrates, soybeans are also rich in many other chemical compounds and nutrients. Although these compounds make up only a small portion of the soybean, they play an important nutritional role.

The major minerals in soybeans are potassium, sodium, calcium, magnesium, sulfur, and phosphorus. The mineral content can vary widely due to both the type of soil and growing conditions for the soybean.

Although soybeans are not considered to be very rich sources of any one particular vitamin, they do contain vitamins and contribute to overall nutritional well-being. The water-soluble vitamins in soybeans are thiamine, riboflavin, niacin, pantothenic acid, biotin, folic acid, inositol, and choline. Fat-soluble vitamins present in soybeans are vitamins A and E. Vitamin A is in the form of beta carotene and is present in higher levels in immature green soybeans than mature soybeans. Vitamin E is an important antioxidant that protects the body from damaging pollutants and tumor growth.

Phytochemicals: It should come as no surprise to anyone that plants contain powerful chemicals which can have a profound effect on an individual's health or well-being. Many of the drugs used in Western medicine today originate from plant sources. Traditional medicines, such as those used by the Chinese and other Asian peoples, as well as by herbalists and homeopaths, all have their roots in plant sources.

The term phytochemicals is used to describe a class of chemicals derived from plants, including soybeans. In fact, soybeans contain a virtual pharmacy of compounds believed to help prevent certain diseases. However, over the past few years one particular set of compounds has gained the most attention and become the focus of hundreds of studies—isoflavones. Isoflavones are also referred to as phytoestrogens, meaning plant estrogens, because of their similar chemical make-up and effect on the human body. Not only are isoflavones believed to have a positive affect on health, but for all practical purposes, no other food contains significant amounts of these chemicals except soybeans.

The major isoflavones in soybeans are genistein, daidzein, and glycitein, but it is the first two which have become the focus of nutrition research. Of these, it is thought that genistein has the most potential to prevent or treat certain cancers.

Processing soybeans into various food products alters or removes some of these compounds, but for the most part, the simpler the processing involved, the higher the level of isoflavones that remain. For example, foods such as full-fat soy flour, tofu, and soymilk all contain higher levels of isoflavones than isolated soy proteins or soybean concentrates.

Soybeans and Health

Over the past few decades, it has become apparent to most people that there is a simple, yet profound, connection between one's diet and health that simply cannot be dismissed. This conclusion can be made based upon an ever-increasing number of analyses and clinical studies which have been made public over the past few years in medical journals, newspapers, magazines, and on television.

The focus of many of these studies has been on soybeans. This is due to the growing amount of data that has been collected on the health benefits associated with eating soybean-based foods and an increased understanding about which components of the soybean may be responsible for these effects.

In 1994, the first international symposium on the potential role of soyfoods in the prevention and treatment of chronic disease was held in Mesa, Arizona. The conference brought together researchers from around the world who presented data on the soybean's effect on heart disease, cholesterol reduction, cancer prevention, kidney disease, and reduction of menopausal symptoms. The first gathering was so significant that a second symposium was held in 1996 in Brussels, Belgium. During this conference, new evidence was brought forward which not only supported the conclusion of many of the earlier studies, but also presented new, stronger evidence regarding the ability of estrogen-like compounds in soybeans to reduce the symptoms of osteoporosis. It also delved further into the actual mechanism of how soy isoflavones effect health.

Malnutrition

One of the major contributing factors to disease in the world today is malnutrition, or the lack of adequate nutrition. In the developed nations of the world, we have the fortunate luxury of being able to prevent many of our chronic diseases by simply reducing the amount of calories we consume or by changing the types of food we eat. For millions of people in developing nations, there simply is no choice.

According to estimates from the United Nations' Food and Agricultural Organization (FAO) in 1997, there are more than 800 million chronically undernourished people in the developing world today, and 200 million of them are children under the age of five. There are many reasons for this situation and no easy solutions. Politics, war, weather, and inadequate means for distributing goods and services all factor in the creation of hunger on this massive scale.

Malnutrition not only means that people are hungry, it also means that large segments of the population are chronically ill or debilitated and unable to become educated, self-reliant, or productive members of a society. Malnutrition keeps countries dependent on foreign aid and undermines the soul of a nation.

Currently, total world food production just barely keeps up with our growing population. In 1997, our planet's food supply was projected to increase by just 1.1 percent, down from the 3.6 percent rise in 1996 and 1995, and below the world's population growth rate of 1.45 percent a year.

When you consider just how tenuous this situation is, it's easy to see how important the soybean can be to the feeding of humankind. Acreage planted in soybeans will yield at least twice as much protein than if planted with any other major vegetable or grain crop, 5 to 10 times more protein than land set aside for dairy cattle, and up to 15 times more protein than land set aside for beef cattle.

Adding soy protein to breads, tortillas, cornmeal, pasta, milk, or any traditional food is a low-cost, efficient way to ensure adequate nutrition for people who have special dietary needs, such as children, pregnant women, and the elderly. In this manner, not only do people receive enough protein for the development and maintenance of their health, but they also get the added benefits of disease-preventing isoflavones and other phytochemicals.

Cardiovascular Disease

In America, it is estimated that more than 57 million people currently have one or more forms of cardiovascular disease. In addition, heart disease will claim nearly one million lives this year, or about 42 percent of all deaths. And despite major surgical breakthroughs and powerful new drugs, heart disease still kills more people in the United States than does any other ailment. The really sad part of all of this is that most of these deaths are avoidable, as heart disease is closely related to the diet and lifestyle choices we make.

Every few years, it seems, medical research brings more information to light on a particular component of food and its impact on cardiovascular health. We have learned of the importance of reducing our total intake of fat and how to choose fats and oils which are more healthful for us so that we can maintain beneficial cholesterol levels. We also know that certain dietary fibers can help reduce our cholesterol levels.

Recently, however, new information has come out regarding heart disease and the foods we eat—the clear connection between the type of protein we consume and the body's ability to lower and maintain healthful levels of cholesterol and overall cardiovascular health.

Medical researchers have known for some time that animal proteins such as those found in meat, dairy products, and eggs can induce atherosclerosis, or hardening of the arteries, while plant proteins appear to have somewhat of an opposite effect. Although this information seems quite important, it has been overshadowed for years due to the large number of studies which have been publicized regarding cholesterol and fat consumption.

This changed in 1995 when a compilation and summary of numerous past studies, entitled "Health Benefits of Soy Protein," written by Dr. James Anderson of the University of Kentucky, was published in the prestigious *New England Journal of Medicine*. The study's findings were widely reported in the popular press and sent consumers in the U.S. rushing to stores looking for these miracle soyfoods.

Dr. Anderson's study found that soy protein intake was associated with a 9.3 percent reduction in serum cholesterol, a 12.9 percent reduction in LDL cholesterol, and a 10.5 percent reduction in serum triglycerides. Concentrations of HDL, the "good" cholesterol, increased by 2.4 percent. It is estimated that this change in serum cholesterol levels has the potential to reduce risk for coronary artery disease by 18 to 28 percent. Based on the findings from 34 out of the 38 studies reviewed, Dr. Anderson concluded that soy protein was clearly effective in decreasing LDL cholesterol levels.

But the positive effect of soybeans on heart health is not solely due to soy protein and its related compounds; the fats which are found naturally in soybeans also can contribute to a reduction in cholesterol levels.

It is now understood that oils which are high in unsaturated fatty acids, such as soybean oil, tend to decrease total serum cholesterol levels. Soybean oil contains about 50 percent linoleic acid, an essential polyunsaturated fat. In addition, soybean oil also contains about 8 percent linolenic acid, an omega-3 fatty acid that is found mainly in fish oils. This fatty acid has been the subject of numerous studies which link its consumption with a decreased incidence of heart disease and cancer. Soybeans are one of the few plant sources of omega-3 fatty acids.

In addition to the protein and fat, there are a number of other components in soybeans which are believed to be helpful in reducing heart disease. In two separate studies, soy fiber was shown to reduce total cholesterol levels by 5 to 11 percent. Lecithin, which is found in whole soybean-based foods and in unrefined soybean oil, has been shown to reduce cholesterol levels by between 15 and 30 percent. In addition, soybean isoflavone compounds are believed to exert their own downward effect on total cholesterol levels.

It is easy to see how soyfoods can have a major beneficial effect on the health of an individual's cardiovascular system and can play an important role in the reduction of heart disease.

Cancer

As a contributing factor to death in the United States today, cancer trails just behind heart disease. But if researchers at the National Cancer Institute are correct, by the year 2010, cancer will become the leading cause of death in the U.S. It is now estimated that about one out of three Americans will eventually contract cancer, and about one in five will die from it.

Cancer is not an inevitable disease though, as studies in other countries prove. Cancer rates vary considerably among the people of the world, as do the types of cancers that people contract.

In certain epidemiological studies that looked at the incidence of disease in various population groups, soyfoods were originally considered by researchers to be a possible key to disease prevention. For example, in Japan breast cancer rates for woman are about 25 percent of what they are in the U.S.

At a conference convened by the National Cancer Institute in Washington, D.C., in 1990, researchers and experts acknowledged there was strong evidence that soyfoods may play a role in preventing cancer. They identified five specific compounds in soybeans which may be protective: protease inhibitors, phytate, phytosterols, saponins, and isoflavones.

Since 1990, there have been literally thousands of studies conducted by researchers around the world hoping to identify which of these compounds may be the most valuable in the fight against cancer. And although it is not yet certain which one of these compounds is the most important, or if in fact some or all of them work together to a certain extent, many researchers believe that it is the isoflavones which are responsible for much of the anticancer effect. Interestingly enough, soybeans are one of the only regularly consumed foods which contain a significant amount of isoflavones.

There are a number of different compounds in soybeans which are classified as isoflavones, and two in particular have gained the most attention: genistein and daidzein. In their molecular form, isoflavones look very similar to the female sex hormone estrogen, but they are only about 1/100,000 as potent. Because they have a similar structure, they tend to attach to cells in the body in the same way as estrogen does. Even though estrogen is essential for normal bodily function, it can also promote the growth of cancerous tumors. By binding to cells in place of estrogen, soybean phytoestrogens act as protective "anti-estrogens."

Isoflavones are not just beneficial to women. It is possible that they may also have a therapeutic effect for men with prostate cancer, as estrogen has been shown to be an effective therapy for treating that cancer. Prostate cancer has become a major health concern for American men today. According to American Cancer Society estimates, 209,900 new cases will be diagnosed in 1997 and 41,800 men will die from it. In one soyfoods-related study, men who consumed tofu five times per week appeared to be about one-third as likely to develop prostate cancer as those who ate tofu once per week or less.

In experiments on human prostate cancer cells, genistein has been shown to inhibit cell proliferation. And in addition, genistein has been shown to inhibit angiogenesis, or new tumor growth, thereby slowing the progression of existing cancer.

Isoflavone compounds continue to be the subject of hundreds of ongoing clinical studies, some of which are showing very favorable results—not just for cancer, but also for the treatment of heart disease and osteoporosis.

Because isoflavones are present in soybeans in large quantities, just one serving of soyfoods a day may be enough to reduce the risk of certain cancers. One serving is equal to one cup of soymilk, ½ cup of cooked soybeans, ¾ cup of tofu, three ounces of tempeh, or ½ cup of reconstituted textured soy protein.

It is exciting to think that just by eating soybeans, we can reduce the risk of this major killer. According to noted researcher and author Dr. Mark Messina, "although certainly speculative, this is the area where soyfoods may have their greatest impact in public health."

Osteoporosis

Osteoporosis is rapidly becoming a major health problem in the United States and many other countries around the world. In the U.S. alone, it is estimated that between 15 and 20 million people have this disease. Consumption of soyfoods may help to maintain and even rebuild bone density and strength and act as an effective treatment for osteoporosis.

Studies have shown that diets high in animal protein tend to cause calcium to be leached from the bones and excreted in the urine and feces. On the other hand, the protein from soybeans does not cause this to happen.

Also, one of the isoflavones in soybeans, daidzein, is very similar to the drug ipriflavone, which is currently being used in Europe and Asia to treat osteoporosis. As this drug becomes metabolized in the body, daidzein is one of the substances that is produced. Other studies have shown that the isoflavone genistein inhibits bone breakdown and may increase bone density as well. In 1996, it was reported that in a six-month clinical study, post-menopausal women who consumed 40 grams of isolated soy protein a day (which contained 2.25 mg of isoflavones per gram) significantly increased their bone mineral density.

Much attention has been focused on the need to increase calcium intake to help prevent osteoporosis, and most people tend to think of dairy products as the best source for calcium. But many soyfoods are naturally rich in calcium, and the calcium from soyfoods is absorbed as well as that which comes from milk. Good sources of calcium are tofu (in particular, tofu which has been coagulated with calcium sulfate), calcium-fortified soymilk, whole soybeans, soy flour, and tempeh.

Menopause

With the aging of the baby boom generation in America, many woman are already, or will soon be, experiencing the many symptoms related to menopause, which may include hot flashes. Could soyfoods, with their estrogenic isoflavone compounds, help to reduce the severity or frequency of hot flashes? This question has been the focus of numerous studies since 1990, and although some of the studies have been inconclusive, much of the data have shown positive results. One study reported that hot flashes, night sweats, and overall symptoms decreased by 40 percent over a period of several weeks when the women ate 45 grams of raw soy flour per day. In another study, woman who ate 20 grams of soy protein a day containing 34 mg of isoflavones experienced a modest, but statistically significant, decrease in the severity of symptoms (although not a decrease in the frequency).

It would seem to make sense, then, that even without truly conclusive data related to the relief of menopausal symptoms, woman still stand to gain much from the consumption of soyfoods. The combination of health benefits related to heart disease, cancer, and osteoporosis, as well as possible relief from the symptoms of menopause, indicate that soyfoods may be a possible natural substitute for hormone replacement therapy.

Still More to Come

It's apparent that soybeans and the foods made from them can exert a very positive effect on our health. But there is still much more to learn about human nutrition and the role of foods and environment in maintaining health. Fortunately, research on soybeans and soyfoods has accelerated at a phenomenal rate recently, and we will be seeing much more definitive information about the role of soyfoods in the prevention and treatment of disease in the very near future. For men, women, and children, soybeans appear to be one of nature's most nutritious food sources.

Using Soyfoods

Whole Dry Soybeans

 Whole dry soybeans, are the original soyfood. There is a difference in composition between different varieties of soybeans—some seeds are larger in size and higher in protein than others. Dried yellow soybeans are the most commonly available type, though black varieties may also be found.

When making soyfoods, processors select the appropriate variety for the type of product they are making. For example, soymilk and tofu manufacturers like to select large, high-protein soybeans so they'll get a good yield after processing and their products will have a mild flavor.

Common yellow soybeans can be found prepackaged or in bulk in many natural food stores. When buying soybeans, look for beans that are mostly whole and have a minimum of split seeds. Split soybeans will not only soak at different rates than whole beans, but they also will create more off-flavors as a result of oxidation during soaking. Buy clean soybeans, with no dirt or foreign matter such as stones, pods, or other grain such as corn. If you do buy soybeans that are dirty, be sure to rinse them well before using, and remove any stones or pods.

Dried soybeans will last over a year, but they do begin to degrade when stored at too high a temperature or in moist conditions. Keep them cool and dry for best results.

Most recipes call for soaking soybeans before cooking. Soak soybeans in cool, clean water for 8 to 12 hours, or for less time in warmer water. Soybeans will absorb almost 1½ times their weight in water and will come apart easily when completely soaked. The two sides of the soybean will be flat and smooth on the inside. If they are still concave, they have not soaked long enough. If you soak soybeans too long, foam may begin to form on the water, and off-odors may develop. If you need to store soaked soybeans for a short period of time, rinse them and refrigerate until ready to use. If you like, the hulls can be removed easily by rubbing the beans gently between your fingers after soaking. The hulls will float in water and can be skimmed off.

If you are going to cook whole soybeans, the best method is in a pressure cooker for 1 to 2 hours at 15 pounds pressure. You can also boil them in water on your stove top for 7 to 9 hours, though this may still not get them to a soft, easy-to-mash state.

Tofu

Tofu is perhaps the most widely consumed soyfood in the world today. It is a regular part of the diet in many Asian nations and is available across the United States and in most Western nations. This soft, white, almost cheese-like product is favored for its versatility, mild flavor, and high nutritional value. It is naturally processed from whole soybeans and, as a result, retains a good deal of the soybean's important nutrients and phytochemicals, such as isoflavones.

What makes tofu such an exciting food for cooks is its ability to take on the flavor of whatever spices and ingredients are used to prepare it. For example, in the same sitting, one could dine on a fresh green salad served with a creamy tofu dill dressing, eat a hearty serving of marinated barbecued tofu, and finish with a tofu chocolate cream pie.

Tofu is available in a variety of styles and in a number of different types of packaging. It is sold in supermarkets (either in the produce or dairy case) and in natural food stores, co-ops, and Asian markets.

To make tofu, whole, soaked soybeans are ground to produce a slurry, which is added to water and boiled. After cooking, the pulp is removed from the mixture, and what is left is soymilk. While the soymilk is still hot, a natural mineral coagulant, such as calcium sulfate, magnesium chloride, or a mixture of both, is added slowly to the hot liquid. Within minutes, the soymilk begins to curdle, and large, white clouds of tofu curd begin to form in a sea of yellow whey. After 15 minutes or so, the curds are removed from the whey and placed in cloth-lined containers. The curds are then pressed to form soft, regular, firm, or extra-firm tofu. The size of the curd and length of the pressing time determines the style of tofu made. The softer the tofu, the lower the protein and fat level and higher the water content. Soft tofu is usually smoother in texture than firm tofu. Firm tofu, on the other hand, is higher in protein and fat, lower in moisture, and will have a denser, chewier texture.

Silken tofu is a soft, smooth variety commonly sold in an aseptic package or, occasionally, in a tub. To make silken tofu, either calcium sulfate or glucono-delta-lactone is added to a thicker, richer soymilk than is used to make regular tofu, and the mixture is poured into a package. This package, with the soymilk and coagulant mixture, is heated to the proper temperature to activate the coagulation, and the soymilk is transformed into one solid, smooth curd, right in the package.

Typically, tofu contains between 10 and 15 percent protein and 5 to 9 percent fat. It is relatively low in carbohydrates, as well as fiber, making it easy to digest. If you are concerned about getting extra calcium in your diet, look for tofu made with calcium sulfate or calcium chloride, as these products will typically contain higher levels of calcium. One 4-ounce serving of tofu coagulated with calcium can contain as much usable calcium as one 8-ounce serving of cow's milk.

Tofu is commonly found packed in sealed, water-filled tubs, but is also available in vacuum or aseptic packaging. Except for the asceptically-packed tofu (sterilized in the package), all tofu requires refrigeration at or under 40°F. (Look for "sell by" or "use by" dates on the package.) Tofu is usually sold in 12- or 16-ounce packages. If you buy bulk tofu from an open bucket in a food co-op, natural food store, or Asian food market, be sure to store the tofu in a container of water in your refrigerator, change the water daily, and use all the tofu within a few days. Also, once you open a sealed package of tofu, even the asceptically packed variety, store any leftover tofu in fresh, cold water in your refrigerator and use within a few days. Tofu can also be frozen for longer storage, although the tofu will tend to have a much different texture when thawed.

When using tofu in recipes, be sure to select the right style or density of tofu for the dish (although most types are somewhat interchangeable depending on the recipe). As you become more experienced in using tofu, you will know if you need to adjust your recipes by adding or reducing any moist ingredients and/or water in the dish to accommodate the type of tofu you're using.

Regular pressed tofu is best used in frying, baking, grilling, barbecuing, in stir-fry dishes, and as a meat alternative. In most cases, the best way to prepare tofu for use is to first drain the block or tofu slices on paper or cloth towels to reduce the water content. This will improve the tofu's ability to absorb flavors, reduce the amount of water it will release when cooked, and make it firmer and easier to handle.

Thawed, frozen tofu will act more like a sponge than regular tofu (and looks like one too!) and has a much chewier texture and slightly yellow color. It is great as a ground meat replacer in pasta sauce, sloppy Joes, and chili.

Silken tofu is best used in soups or blended into vegetable spreads, sauces, cream substitutes, pie fillings, puddings, or desserts. There are some firm varieties of silken tofu available as well, and these can be used the same way as pressed tofu in many recipes. The Japanese favor silken tofu; they usually prepare it very simply and serve it fresh, with just a little soy sauce and scallions or in miso soup. Silken tofu is a little more difficult to handle than regular or pressed tofu, as it is soft and lacks the same amount of cohesiveness.

Soymilk

Until recently, all soymilk was made by cooking ground, soaked soybeans in water, then straining off the resulting milk. But the beverage-quality soymilks available today are usually prepared in a slightly different fashion, utilizing a number of more "modern" food processing techniques in order to produce a blander product with greater taste appeal. Also, over 90 percent of the soymilk sold in Western nations today is packaged in aseptic cartons, giving the product a nonrefrigerated shelf-life of up to one year.

As with tofu, traditionally processed soymilk will contain most of the active phytochemicals present in soybeans, including high amounts of isoflavones. There are also a number of soymilks available which are fortified with vitamins and minerals, such as beta-carotene and calcium.

Soymilk is usually labeled as "soy drink" or "soy beverage" in the U.S. because the U.S. Food and Drug Administration, the government agency which regulates food labeling, requested that manufacturers not use the term "milk" in association with soymilk. Hopefully this will change in the future, as the Soyfoods Association of North America filed a petition with the FDA in February of 1997 requesting that they develop a regulation allowing the use of the term "soymilk" for this type of product. In the meantime, don't be surprised if the soymilk you buy is called "soy drink."

It is a good idea to compare the protein and fat level of the soymilk you purchase with other brands. Because there has been no industry standard for soymilk, you will find a wide range of nutrients depending on the brand of soymilk you get. The protein level in the leading brands now available ranges from 1½ percent to 4 percent, and the fat will be from 1 percent to 3 percent. If you want the most nutritious products, look for ones with the highest protein levels. The higher the protein level, the higher the phytochemical and isoflavone level, as these components are bound together in the soymilk. Soymilk is also lactose-free, making it an excellent substitute for those who are lactose intolerant. And, as with all soyfoods, soymilk is completely cholesterol-free. A note of caution though: soymilk should not be used as a substitute for infant formula, unless it is specifically labeled for such use.

As mentioned earlier, most of the soymilk available today is found in aseptic packaging which does not require refrigeration. The soymilk is sterilized and transferred into sterilized packages. The result is a product that is virtually free of bacteria and other organisms which can cause spoilage. Also, the light barrier in these packages helps to preserve the soymilk's flavor and vitamin content. Soymilk is also available in refrigerated gable-top cartons and in plastic containers. These products have a shorter shelf-life, but are usually sold at a slightly lower price. Be sure to look for "use by" or "sell by" dates when buying soymilk.

Ascetically packaged soymilk could be found in one of any number of locations in a store—in an end aisle display, with the powdered milk products, or anywhere on the grocery shelf. Refrigerated soymilk is usually sold alongside tofu or in the dairy case along with other dairy products.

Soymilk can be used to replace an equal amount of cow's milk in most recipes, but "lite" soymilk products will not be as rich and creamy. Soymilk works very well in baking recipes and is an excellent cream soup or sauce base. It can be put on cereal or made into yogurt, pudding, or ice cream. When using soymilk in your coffee, put the soymilk in your cup first to avoid curdling. There are also a number of powdered soymilk products which are excellent. If you need a very thick, cream-like soymilk in recipes, mix these powdered milks with less water than you would usually use to make soymilk for drinking.

Soy Flour

Soy flour is available in a number of different forms, but consumers will most likely find two varieties: full-fat and defatted (low-fat). Another form, textured soy protein, is not actually a flour, but a quick-cooking meat substitute made from defatted soy flour.

Full-Fat Soy Flour: Full-fat soy flour is made from whole or dehulled soybeans that have been ground into a fine flour. Its composition is identical to that of whole soybeans, with a protein content of between 35 and 40 percent and a fat level of between 15 to 20 percent. It is extremely nutritious, high in fiber, and contains all of the soybean's vitamins, minerals, and phytochemicals.

Full-fat soy flour is available either as a raw flour (enzyme-active) or as a toasted flour. The raw form is great for baking, as the active enzyme lipoxygenase helps to bleach whole wheat flour and produce a moist, white loaf of bread that will not go stale quickly. The toasted variety will have a somewhat nuttier flavor and slightly darker color.

You will most likely find soy flour in a natural food store or co-op, as it is not usually found in supermarkets. There may be some baking flour mixes available which contain soy flour in them, so look for these. Because of its high oil content, it is a good idea to keep full-fat soy flour refrigerated.

Full-fat soy flour can be used in bread, muffins, pancakes, cookies, and most other recipes calling for wheat flour. Depending on the recipe, you should be able to substitute anywhere from 5 to 15 percent of the wheat flour with soy. Start with a 5 percent substitution and increase it very slightly each time you prepare the recipe to see just how much soy flour you can use before it adversely affects the yield, color, or taste. Also, remember to adjust the amount of any oil you would add to the recipe to compensate for the fat which occurs naturally in the full-fat soy flour.

Enzyme-active full-fat soy flour can also be used to make fresh soymilk without having to soak or grind soybeans. Check for the recipe on page 31 of the Basics chapter.

Defatted Soy Flour: Defatted soy flour, sometimes referred to as simply "soy flour," is made by finely grinding defatted soybean flakes. Defatted flakes are produced by flaking soybeans in a roller mill and then removing the soybean oil with a solvent. (Defatted soy grits are processed in the same manner but not ground as finely). Typically, defatted soy flour has a higher proportion of protein than full-fat soy flour because it has less fat. It contains between 44 to 54 percent protein, 0.5 to 1.0

percent fat, 17 to 18 percent dietary fiber, and 30 to 35 percent total carbohydrates.

There are also low-fat soy flours available which are made from soybeans that have been mechanically pressed to remove the oil prior to grinding. Because mechanical extraction of the oil is not as efficient as solvent extraction, these products will typically contain more fat than other defatted flours (between 7 and 10 percent), so their protein content will range from 45 to 50 percent.

Defatted soy flour contains more isoflavone compounds than both whole soybeans and products produced with them, because it has a higher proportion of protein. Some of the nutrients found in the oil, such as vitamin E and lecithin, will be removed in the defatting process, but most of the vitamins, minerals, fiber, and phytochemicals are retained.

Defatted soy flours are very useful in baking and, as with full-fat flours, can be substituted for anywhere from 5 to 15 percent of other flours in a recipe. Defatted soy flour can be found in natural food stores, co-ops, and some supermarkets. It's not quite as perishable as full-fat soy flour, but you should refrigerate it to reduce any oxidation which can create off flavors.

Textured Soy Protein

Textured soy protein is processed from very low-fat (defatted) soy flour. It is available in a range of colors, shapes, and sizes and is most commonly used as a meat extender or replacement due to its meat-like appearance and consistency. This product is nutritionally equivalent to regular defatted soy flour and is a great source of protein, fiber, and isoflavones.

To make textured soy protein, defatted soy flour is mixed with water and then cooked under high pressure in an extruder to produce a variety of textured and shaped products. The extrusion process produces the unique texture by expanding the structure of the soy protein. A die at the end of the extruder determines the shape and size of the piece or granule. Flavor or color can be added to the soy flour prior to processing.

To use textured soy protein in recipes, you must first add hot or boiling water to the granules. As the textured soy protein absorbs the water, it expands and softens. Once it's fully hydrated, drain off any remaining water and use in recipes much the same as you would ground meat. Textured soy protein can replace all the meat in a recipe.

As there is virtually no fat in textured soy protein, you might want to add some vegetable oil to certain recipes to help to enhance flavors. Unlike ground meat, reconstituted textured soy protein will stick to the pan when fried unless you add oil and/or use a nonstick pan. You can also brown the dry granules before adding water.

The U. S. Department of Agriculture recently adopted new rules for its school lunch program which allows school cafeterias to substitute 30 percent of ground meat in most recipes with fortified textured soy protein and 100 percent of ground meat if they use non-fortified soy protein as part of their "Nu Menus" program. If you'd like more information on how your school can use textured soy protein in its lunch program, contact the American School Food Service Association in Alexandria, Virginia, at 1-800-877-8822, or the United Soybean Board at 1-800-TALKSOY.

Textured soy protein can be purchased in bulk or in prepackaged containers in natural food stores, co-ops, by mail order, and in some supermarkets. If kept in a dry, tightly closed container, it will keep for months without refrigeration.

Green Vegetable Soybeans

Green soybeans are whole soybeans picked at the peak of maturity, when they are high in sucrose and chlorophyll and have a firm texture. They are harvested in the pod and sold either in the pod or shucked after being blanched and frozen. Because they are picked when their sugar levels are high, green vegetable soybeans are very sweet and pleasant tasting. The common, traditional Japanese name for green vegetable soybeans is "edamame," when sold in the pod, and "mukimame," when sold as individual beans.

Green vegetable soybeans contain about 13 percent protein, the same amount as tofu, and are naturally high in calcium. They work very well in stir-fry dishes and can also be blended into dips and other preparations. They are not easy to find in this country, being available primarily in Asian markets, but are now making their way into natural food stores and supermarkets. Keep them frozen until use. Of course, you can also grow them in your home garden! If you grow your own, you can use them fresh out of the garden, or blanch them in boiling water for just a few seconds prior to freezing.

Tempeh

Tempeh is a delicious, fermented soyfood that has a variety of uses. Originating in Indonesia, tempeh has a distinctive flavor, sometimes described as "nutty" or "mushroom-like," and a texture similar to green soybeans. It is made from whole soybeans which have been dehulled, cracked, and cooked in water with a little vinegar. Once cooked, the soybeans are mixed with spores of the Rhizopus oligosporus mold and left to incubate for 24 hours at around 88°F. At the end of this period, the soybeans have become a compact cake, completely covered with and penetrated by the white mold fibers which have formed. Tempeh can also be made by adding in other grains or seeds during processing to vary the taste and texture of the final product. Tempeh contains about 19 percent protein, is higher in fiber than tofu, and is a significant source of vitamins and minerals.

Tempeh can be marinated prior to use. It works very well in stir-fry dishes and can be baked, grilled, or deep-fried. Tempeh can also be grated and formed into patties or balls. Because it is so easy to digest, it is a good food for children and older people. Tempeh is available fresh or frozen and is sold in plain and flavored varieties. It can be found in natural food stores and in many supermarkets in the produce section. Tempeh should be used within a few weeks of purchase, but can be frozen for longer storage.

Miso

Miso is a rich, flavorful paste made from fermented, aged whole soybeans or soybeans in combination with wheat, barley, or rice. This salty paste is a traditional soup base and flavoring ingredient used throughout Japan, Korea, Taiwan, Indonesia, and China. There are many types of miso available, from sweet white miso, which is quite mild, to dark savory miso, which is much more robust and salty.

Miso has unique medicinal properties and is believed to help reduce the effects of radiation and other environmental poisons on the body. It also contains enzymes and bacteria which can aid in digestion. Miso is high in protein, but it also contains a large amount of sodium and should be consumed sparingly.

To make miso, whole cooked soybeans are combined with koji nuggets, a form of wheat, rice, or barley which has been cultured with a fungal starter (Aspergillus oryzae) and fermented under very specific conditions for the type of miso being made. When the mash is fully ripened, it is blended and packaged for sale. Most of the miso sold today is pasteurized, though some brands are sold unpasteurized and refrigerated.

Miso is sold in natural food stores and in some supermarkets along with other Oriental foods and has a long shelf life when refrigerated. Because there are many varieties available, be sure to try different types so you can experience the differences in flavor. Usually the longer the miso has aged, the more complex flavor it has.

The most common way miso is used is as a broth or soup base—start with one tablespoon or so per cup of water. Be careful not to boil the soup after adding miso, as this destroys any beneficial bacteria or enzymes the miso contains. Because it is a fermented product, it will add a cheese-like flavor to many of the foods it's added to, such as blended tofu.

Soy Sauce

Soy sauce is the most well known and popular traditional soyfood and is used extensively as a flavoring ingredient in Oriental cooking. Naturally processed soy sauce is made by a natural fermentation process similar to miso. When made exclusively with soybeans, the product is called tamari. If it is processed with a fermented wheat starter, the product is called shoyu. Much of the soy sauce sold today is made with hydrolyzed vegetable protein, or HVP, with added sugar, color and preservatives. HVP is produced from soy protein using a chemically-induced fermentation. All soy sauces are high in sodium and should be used sparingly. There are some reduced-sodium varieties on the market today, as well as a number of flavored soy sauce products.

From a nutritional perspective, tamari contains the highest protein level of the soy sauces, followed by shoyu and HVP-based soy sauce. But the high amount of sodium in all of these products should preclude anyone from using soy sauce as a source of protein.

Soy sauce is available in its more natural forms in natural food stores and in both the naturally fermented and HVP forms in most supermarkets.

Due to its high salt content, soy sauce has a long shelf life without refrigeration, but will keep longer when stored at cooler temperatures.

Soybean Protein Concentrate

Soy protein concentrate is not a product that one is likely to find in a grocery store, but it is used extensively in soy-based meat and dairy alternatives. It contains between 65 and 70 percent soy protein, a trace amount of fat, and a good deal of fiber. It is made by processing defatted soybean flakes in either an alcohol or water bath to remove soluble sugars. The result is a concentrated form of soy flour which is tastier and easier to process than defatted flour. It can be texturized (the most common way it's used in meat substitutes) or spray-dried to form a powder used in infant formulas and other dairy substitutes. Due to the alcohol processing used to reduce the sugars, most of the valuable isoflavones are removed, though the quality of the protein is not reduced at all. It is also more easily digested than soy flour, as most of the sugars responsible for creating flatulence have been removed during processing.

As mentioned earlier, you're not likely to find a product labeled "soy protein concentrate" in a store, you'll find it listed on the label of many soy-based meat alternatives, along with the term "textured soy protein concentrate."

Soy Protein Isolates

Isolated soy protein is essentially pure soybean protein processed from the same defatted soy flakes as defatted soy flour and soy protein concentrate. When making isolated soy protein, the processing is taken one step further to remove not only the fat and soluble sugars, but also the insoluble sugars and dietary fiber. What remains is 90 percent pure protein, some residual minerals, and a trace amount of fat. Isolated soy proteins are very low in flavor, highly digestible, and easy to add to your favorite drinks and recipes. Soy isolate disperses easily in water and works well as an emulsifier, helping to bind water and fat together.

Until recently, soy protein isolate did not contain many of the valuable isoflavones, as they were lost during processing. But recently, newer processing techniques have been developed, and many isolated soy protein products, specifically those designed for human consumption, contain high levels of isoflavones.

Isolated soy protein is found in many of the meat and dairy alternatives in the market today. They are also used with whole soybeans to make certain types of tofu, blended with tofu in tofu hot dogs to improve the texture, used in some soymilk products in place of the whole soybean, and are used in nondairy creamers and infant formulas. They are also found in many of the weight and muscle gain products sold to the fitness market. And due to their highly functional qualities, the meat industry uses isolated soy proteins to help bind water and fat in processed meats and to reduce shrinkage during cooking.

Consumers can now buy isolated soy protein under a variety of brand names and labels, marketed either as a nutritional aid or a food and drink base. They are most likely to be found in natural food or supplement stores or can be purchased through direct mail. Properly stored, they should have a long shelf life with or without refrigeration.

Natto

Natto is a whole soybean product which is very popular in Japan. It is produced by fermenting small, cooked soybeans with Bacillus natto until they develop a sticky, viscous coating. Natto has a strong flavor and aroma and is definitely a treat for the adventurous eater. It is available only in Japanese food stores and is mostly imported, as very little is produced in the U.S. It can be found frozen or fresh and will last about a week if refrigerated.

Soybean Oil

Soybean oil is produced from whole soybeans by means of mechanical or solvent extraction. In the first step of extraction, a crude soybean oil is removed from the soybeans. This is then filtered or refined further to produce what we know as soybean oil and use on our salads or in cooking.

In the U.S., most of the "vegetable oil" we see in grocery stores is really pure soybean oil. In other countries, it is labeled as soybean oil or soya oil. It is the primary oil used in the food processing industry and is found in vegetable oil shortenings and margarine.

Like any oil, soybean oil is 100 percent fat, but it is high in polyunsaturated fats, low in saturated fats, and a good source of linoleic and linolenic acids, the heart-protective omega-3 and omega-6 fatty acids also found in fish oils.

Much of the soybean oil sold today is either hydrogenated or partially hydrogenated. There are numerous studies now underway to determine if this form of fat and the trans-fatty acids produced with them, are detrimental or not to a person's cardiac health. Preliminary evidence suggests that hydrogenated soybean oil is not a healthful fat, so you might want to limit your intake until more information is available. Non-hydrogenated liquid soybean oil will not contain these controversial trans-fatty acids.

Second Generation Soyfoods

Soyfoods companies have been very responsive to consumer trends and are aware that in addition to choosing foods for value and health reasons, shoppers also buy for convenience. As a result, a wide array of "second generation" soyfoods are available in the marketplace today, catering to just about anyone's particular taste and use preferences. For example, one can now find tofu-stuffed pasta, as well as tofu-based dips, dressings, and puddings. Soymilk is made into yogurt, ice cream, and cheese. Tempeh and tofu are now available flavored, marinated, baked, or smoked. Pizza is topped with soy cheese, and textured soy concentrate is mixed with gluten to form a ground meat alternative. Hundreds of products are now available for just about any recipe application. Many of these products are available in supermarkets in their specialty grocery sections or produce departments, and, of course, in natural foods stores. Ask the store manager where you shop about the products that he or she can order.

Meat Alternatives

This is an exciting product category with literally hundreds of products now available made from tofu, tempeh, textured soy flour, textured soy concentrate, and isolated soy protein. Products take the shape of burgers, hot dogs, sausages, luncheon meats, ground meat, and meat balls. Most products are made with a combination of vegetable protein ingredients to achieve the best texture and are flavored for a particular use. Most are low in fat and many are completely fat-free.

Products are sold fresh and frozen and can be purchased in most natural food stores and many supermarkets. They can be used simply as is or as a replacement for meat in recipes. They require much less cooking time than meat products, so be careful not to overcook them.

Cheese Alternatives

There is now a wide range of block, sliced, spreadable, and grated cheese alternatives made with soymilk, tofu, and other vegetable protein ingredients. They can be found flavored like American cheese, mozzarella, cheddar, Monterey Jack, Parmesan, and others. Most of these products are made with casein, a protein derived from cow's milk. The protein in casein allows cheese to melt when heated. Without casein, the soy cheese alternatives would just soften, but not melt or stretch. Casein also adds a "dairy-like" flavor which is associated with cheese products. There are some products available with no casein at all, so look for these products if you are a vegan or need a dairy-free alternative.

Soy-based cheese alternatives contain vegetable oils instead of butterfat, and, in some cases, all the fat has been completely removed. They are lactose- and cholesterol-free as well. Some supermarkets now carry these products in the produce or dairy case, and most natural food stores carry more than one brand. After opening, they can last up to a few months in the refrigerator and can be used in just about any recipe calling for cheese, including pizza, Mexican food, and desserts.

Soy cheese alternatives are also used as an ingredient in prepared frozen pizza, stuffed in pasta, and added to frozen entrees.

Soy Yogurt

Soy yogurt is made in the same manner as dairy yogurt. Pasteurized soymilk is inoculated with acidophilus, bifidus, or other suitable cultures and incubated until the culture has turned the soymilk into yogurt. It tastes very similar to dairy yogurt and is available in a variety of styles and flavors. It is sold in 6- to 8-ounce single-serving containers and one-quart tubs, mostly in natural food stores. You probably will not see these products labeled as "yogurt." Since they are not made with cow's milk, the manufacturers are not allowed to legally label them as such. Look for the same style of containers that dairy yogurt comes in and interesting names such as "soygurt" or cultured soymilk.

Soy yogurt is very high in protein, a great source of isoflavones, and can be used as is or in recipes calling for yogurt.

Nondairy Frozen Desserts

These very important products helped to prove to Americans that foods made from tofu and soybeans could taste good. Popularized by brands such as Tofutti, this category has not grown much over the years due to heavy competition among ice cream products overall, but there are still a number of very good, nutritious products available. Some are high-fat, some are low-fat, and a few are completely fat-free. Look for these in the premium ice cream section of your supermarket or natural food store.

Mayonnaise and Dressings

A popular use of tofu over the years has been as an egg, cream, or mayonnaise replacer. As a result, a number of bottled mayonnaise and creamy salad dressings are now available which use tofu as a base. These are very flavorful, low in fat, and a good way to season up salads, vegetables, and cooking sauces. These products are sold in natural food stores, and many do not require refrigeration until after opening.

Instant Soups and Other Dry Mixes

Instant soups are a very popular product, and many are available with powdered miso or dried tofu. Also, there are a number of dry mixes available which can be added to tofu, stir-fries, or burgers.

Margarine

Margarine is a butter substitute made primarily from an emulsified mixture of oil and water. It may have other ingredients added, such as coloring and non-fat milk solids. The primary oil used in margarine is soybean oil, but it is also made using other oils such as corn, canola, and sunflower. The oil is usually hydrogenated, mixed with water, coloring, and milk or soybean solids, and formed into sticks. There are also softer varieties available which contain varying amounts of oil, water, and solids and are sold in tubs. There is at least one brand available, Willow Run, which is made entirely from soybeans and contains no dairy products. Read margarine labels carefully to see which types of oil are used and what other ingredients the margarine contains.

As most of the oils used to make margarine are partially hydrogenated (which are more saturated and contain trans-fatty acids believed to be unhealthful), try to limit your consumption of margarine to those uses where liquid oil would not be appropriate.

Lecithin

Lecithin is a type of fat which is removed from crude soybean oil during the degumming process. It is an excellent emulsifying agent, used widely in food applications, and is also believed to lower blood cholesterol levels.

Lecithin is available in granular or liquid form, as well as in capsules, and can be purchased in pharmacies, supermarkets, and natural food stores. It is not usually used in home recipes except occasionally as an egg replacer. Eggs naturally contain a high amount of lecithin.

Soynuts and Soynut Butter

Soynuts are whole or split soybeans which have first been soaked in water, then dry- or oil-roasted. They often are sold salted and/or flavored. Soynut pieces can be blended with other nuts and used in baking or added to your favorite recipe. They are high in protein, fiber, and the isoflavones found naturally in whole soybeans.

Soynut butter is a paste of ground soynuts similar to peanut butter and may have salt, sweeteners, and oil added.

Soynuts and soynut butter can be found in many natural food stores and in some supermarkets.

Soy Sprouts

Soy sprouts are the fresh, crisp sprouts of germinated soybeans. They are a traditional food of Korea and eaten either raw or in prepared food dishes. Soy sprouts are usually sold after 5 to 7 days of growth. They are high in protein and fiber and contain vitamin C.

Soy sprouts are slightly larger than ordinary bean sprouts which are usually grown from mung beans. Soy sprouts may be available in some specialty food stores, but they are most likely to be found in Korean grocery stores along with other fresh produce.

Okara or Soy Pulp

Okara is the fibrous pulp that is leftover when making soymilk. It contains the insoluble carbohydrates and dietary fiber of the soybean, as well some remaining protein and fat. Okara will add a nutty flavor and additional nutrients to breads and other baked goods. It can also be used to make meat alternatives and can be processed into tempeh.

Okara is not usually sold in stores, as it is very wet, heavy, and highly perishable. If you make your own soymilk at home or are lucky enough to live near a soymilk manufacturer, you'll have a ready supply.

Basics

Pressure Cooked Soybeans

The protein in soybeans must be thoroughly cooked before it can be digested. Pressure cooking is the best method to fully cook whole dried soybeans. Stovetop cooking does not yield a truly soft bean, even after 9 to 10 hours of cooking. A soybean that is properly cooked will be easily squashed by your tongue on the roof of your mouth.

Soybeans contain some sugars that are not easily digested by some people and can cause gas or flatulence problems for others. Soaking and/or blanching the beans before cooking can help solve this problem. Adding some kombu seaweed to the cooking water can also help. Kombu is a natural flavor enhancer, eliminating the need to add salt.

Yield: 2½ to 3 cups (5 servings)

Soybeans

1 cup dried soybeans
3 cups water
2-inch square piece of kombu (optional)
1 tablespoon oil (optional)

1

Sort and wash the soybeans. They can be cooked with or without soaking. Blanching, quick soaking, or pressure soaking will help eliminate the offending sugars mentioned above.

2

Overnight Soaking: Soak the soybeans overnight in cold water. To blanch the soybeans, add the soaked soybeans to boiling water, and boil for 10 minutes. Drain and rinse.

3

Quick Soaking: Pour boiling water over the soybeans, boil for about 10 minutes, and let stand for about 1 hour. Pour off the water, rinse, and drain.

4

Pressure Soaking: Bring the soybeans and water to full pressure in a pressure cooker; turn off the cooker. Let the pressure drop on its own. Rinse and drain.

5

To cook soaked beans, add fresh water to the pressure cooker, the oil, if using, and cook at 15 pounds pressure for 30 to 40 minutes.

6

Cook unsoaked soybeans at 15 pounds pressure for 45 to 75 minutes. The average cooking time will be about 1 hour, but it will vary depending on the variety, age, and dryness of the beans.

7

The skins of the beans may tend to come loose and clog the pressure cooker vent. If the vent becomes clogged, bring the pressure all the way down, remove the lid, clean out the vent pipe, and skim off any loose bean skins that are floating on top. Reclose the pot, bring to pressure again, and continue cooking. *Never leave your pressure cooker unattended.*

Per serving: Calories 149, Total Protein 12 g, Soy Protein 12 g, Fat 7 g, Carbohydrates 9 g, Calcium 88 mg, Fiber 4 g, Sodium 1 mg

Soybean Sprouts

Crunchy, nutritious, and tasty, soy sprouts are easy to make at home and are sometimes available in Asian or natural foods stores. Soybeans take anywhere from 5 to 10 days to sprout. For the best prices, purchase soybeans in bulk quantities from a food co-op. Make sure the soybeans have not been treated with mercury or other chemicals.

Yield: 1 quart

Soybeans

1

Rinse the soybeans well, about 3 to 4 times, to remove bacteria and dust. Soak the soybeans overnight in lukewarm to cool water to germinate them. If you are sprouting in a jar, soak them in the same jar. Stretch some nylon or cheesecloth over the top of the jar, and secure it with a ring or rubber band. Drain by tilting the jar over a sink. If sprouting on a tray, drain the soybeans thoroughly in a colander, and spread them on the tray.

3

Sprout the soybeans in a warm, dark place. Spread the soybeans no more than 2-inches thick. If you're using a jar, turn it sideways and shake the soybeans so they line the sides of the jar. If you're using a tray, line the bottom with a damp cloth, spread the soybeans, and cover with cheesecloth.

4

Water the sprouting soybeans whenever they look dry (usually 2 to 3 times a day). A spray-mister is a good device to use for watering, especially when growing them on a tray. Soybeans sprouted in a jar can be rinsed under tap water, but they should be thoroughly drained.

Materials:
Dry soybeans (about ¼ cup dry soybeans will fill a quart jar with sprouts)
Waterproof container to grow the sprouts in—a glass jar with nylon or cheesecloth stretched across the top and secured with a rubber band; or a tray or cake pan, preferably glass or anything rustproof
Colander for rinsing sprouting soybeans

5

Full-grown soybean sprouts should be 1½ inches to 2½ inches long. Sprouts that are grown in the dark will be yellow. If the fully grown sprouts are placed in indirect sunlight for a few hours, they will develop chlorophyll and turn green. Before serving, submerge the sprouts in cold water, and agitate slightly. Most of the bean hulls will float to the top where they can be removed. Drain and serve or store in an airtight container or plastic bag in the refrigerator. They will keep refrigerated for a few days.

Per ½ cup: Calories 45, Total Protein 4 g, Soy Protein 4 g, Fat 1 g, Carbohydrates 4 g, Calcium 24 mg, Fiber 1 g, Sodium 5 mg

Soy Yogurt

Soy yogurt is a creamy, tangy treat made using the same process as for dairy yogurt. Making yogurt is a simple process, but it takes some time and preparation. You can make your own soymilk from beans, use soymilk made from soymilk powder, or use aseptically packaged, unflavored soymilk. Soy yogurt will keep for up to two weeks in the refrigerator.

Yield: 1 gallon

Soymilk

1 gallon soymilk
Glass canning jars and lids
Ladle or cup
Stainless steel spoon
Jar tongs
Candy thermometer (optional)
1 cup active or live yogurt or a
    yogurt culture

1

Begin by sterilizing the containers and equipment. Use a pot large enough to hold the jars, lids, ladle or cup (for dipping out the hot soymilk), spoon (for stirring the yogurt starter culture), tongs (for lifting out the hot jars), and thermometer. Cover and steam or boil everything for at least 20 minutes.

2

Heat the milk to boiling while stirring constantly. Remove the jars from the sterilizing pot with the sterilized tongs, setting them right side up on a towel. Pour or ladle the soymilk into the sterilized jars, leaving room to add 1 to 2 tablespoons yogurt starter culture. Put the lids on loosely to cover the jars, but don't seal. Let the soymilk cool to 110°F, or until the jar feels warm to the inside of your wrist but does not burn. You can lift a lid and check the temperature with a sterilized thermometer.

3

Add 1 tablespoon of any plain yogurt with a live culture to each pint of soymilk. Check the carton label to make sure the culture is live. If you would rather not use dairy yogurt as a starter, there are freeze dried vegan yogurt starters available at most health food stores. Follow the package directions to use the right amount. Briskly stir in the starter with the sterilized spoon, and cover tightly with the sterilized lid.

4

Place the jars in a heavy duty portable cooler or foam ice chest (without ice, of course), and close it up tightly. Let the yogurt incubate undisturbed for 2 to 6 hours until set. The yogurt is ready if it separates cleanly and easily from the sides of the jar when gently tilted. Refrigerate the finished yogurt.

5

An alternative method for incubation is to have a heavy quilt laid out and folded in half with a towel in the center to protect it from any drips. Arrange the sealed jars in the center, then fold the quilt evenly over, using clothes pins to secure it. Another method for incubation is to wrap the jars in an electric blanket set on a low setting.

Per cup: Calories 82, Total Protein 7 g, Soy Protein 7 g, Fat 4 g, Carbohydrates 4 g, Calcium 17 mg, Fiber 3 g, Sodium 32 mg

Making Soymilk

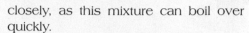

Add ¾ to 1 pound soy flour to 3 quarts water (depending on the desired richness), and boil for 20 to 30 minutes in a heavy-bottomed pot. (If you coat the bottom of the pot with oil before adding the water and soy flour, you'll find clean-up will be easier.)

Be sure to stir constantly and watch closely, as this mixture can boil over quickly.

Reduce foaming by spraying the boiling mixture with cold water from a spray bottle and by stirring. After cooking, strain the soymilk through a cheesecloth-lined colander to remove the residue. Flavor or sweeten as desired.

Frozen Tofu

Tofu

It's convenient to keep frozen tofu on hand. It is easy to defrost at room temperature, in a microwave, or by pouring hot water over the package. It soaks up marinades and has a chewy texture. It's good with vegetables in a won-ton wrapper for an "egg" roll filling, used in

Chinese fried rice or a pot pie, crumbled onto pizza before baking, put in a pot of chili or in a curry sauce. Add it to gravy and serve on rice or mashed potatoes, or enjoy it barbequed. Frozen tofu can be sliced, torn up, or grated on the coarse side of a grater.

Deep Fried Tofu

Tofu

Slice tofu ½ to ¾-inch thick, or cut into cubes. Dry on paper towels.

Fry the tofu until brown and crispy, drain on paper towels, and sprinkle with nutritional yeast flakes, or salt and pepper. Serve with tarter sauce or in sandwiches with salad dressing. Deep Fried Tofu can be basted with barbeque sauce and cooked on a grill, or baked at 350°F for 10 minutes, turn and baste, and cook 10 minutes more.

Quick & Easy Fried Tofu

Perhaps the quickest and easiest way to serve tofu for meals or snacks is to pan fry it. It will take on whatever flavoring is added to it either before or while it is cooking.

Yield: 8 slices

Tofu

2 teaspoons tamari
1 pound firm tofu, cut into 8
　slices
2 tablespoons oil

Seasoning Ingredients:
Garlic powder
Onion powder
Basil
Oregano
Poultry seasoning
Curry powder

1

Place the tamari in a shallow bowl. Dip each slice of tofu in the tamari, then brown on each side in the oil. While the tofu is cooking, sprinkle with any of the seasoning ingredients. Serve with pasta, rice, millet, buckwheat groats, potatoes, or in sandwiches.

Variations: Instead of dipping the slices in tamari, try spreading each slice with a thin layer of Vegemite, Marmite, or miso before frying.

The tofu can also be cut in cubes or crumbled instead of sliced.

Per slice: Calories 74, Total Protein 4 g, Soy Protein 4 g, Fat 6 g, Carbohydrates 1 g, Calcium 60 mg, Fiber 0 g, Sodium 88 mg

Baked Tofu Nuggets

A tasty treat using either frozen or regular tofu.

Yield: 36 nuggets

1

Drain the tofu and slice in half horizontally. Place the two slices on a large plate or cutting board covered with 2 to 3 paper towels. Then place 2 more paper towels on top. Set a heavy cast iron skillet or pan weighted down with a heavy object on top to press the tofu. Let the tofu set for at least 30 minutes.

2

To freeze the tofu, place the two slices of tofu on a rack and place in the freezer. Leave in the freezer about 48 hours. The tofu will take on a yellow to amber color. If you leave the tofu in the freezer longer, place in a freezer bag. To defrost the tofu, place the slices in a large bowl, cover with hot boiling water, and let set for about 10 minutes. Drain the tofu, and press again to remove the remaining water from the tofu. This time press for only 20 minutes.

3

Cut the tofu slices in half, and cut each half in thirds. Turn lengthwise and cut into thirds again. Preheat the oven to 350°F.

1 pound extra-firm tofu
⅛ cup ketchup
2 tablespoons tamari

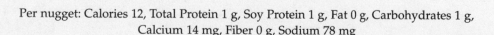

4

Mix the ketchup and tamari. Dip the nuggets completely into the mixture, and place on an oiled cookie sheet. Bake for 20 minutes, turning over once half way through baking.

5

If you don't have the time to freeze the tofu, you can skip the freezing step. Just press the water out of the tofu, cut into cubes, flavor, and bake at 350°F for 30 minutes.

Variation: You can also dip the nuggets into a mixture of equal parts water and tamari, and then dip into crushed almonds.

Per nugget: Calories 12, Total Protein 1 g, Soy Protein 1 g, Fat 0 g, Carbohydrates 1 g, Calcium 14 mg, Fiber 0 g, Sodium 78 mg

Mock Sour Cream Dressing

This low-calorie, no cholesterol dressing can be used in a variety of recipes that call for sour cream.

Yield: 1¼ cups

Tofu

½ pound silken tofu
¼ cup oil
2 tablespoons lemon juice
1½ teaspoons sugar or sweetener
  of your choice (optional)
½ teaspoon salt

1

Combine all the ingredients in a food processor or blender, and blend until smooth and creamy.

Per tablespoon: Calories 33, Total Protein 1 g, Soy Protein 1 g, Fat 3 g, Carbohydrates 0 g, Calcium 12 mg, Fiber 0 g, Sodium 54 mg

Tofu "Ricotta Cheese"

Yield: 1 generous cup

Tofu

½ pound medium-firm tofu,
  mashed and drained
3 tablespoons reduced-fat
  soymilk
¼ teaspoon salt

1

Mix all the ingredients together in a bowl and refrigerate.

Note: This recipe works best with very fresh tofu.

Per ¼ cup: Calories 61, Total Protein 6 g, Soy Protein 6 g, Fat 3 g, Carbohydrates 3 g, Calcium 1 mg, Fiber 1 g, Sodium 141 mg

Breakfast

Apple Juice Pancakes

Yield: 14 to 16 pancakes

Soy Isolate

Dry Ingredients:
1 cup unbleached white flour
¾ cup soy protein isolate
⅔ cup whole wheat pastry flour
½ cup cornmeal
2 teaspoons baking powder
½ teaspoon salt

3 tablespoons canola oil
2½ cups apple juice or cider

1

In a medium mixing bowl, stir together the dry ingredients.

2

Add the oil and apple juice, and mix into the dry ingredients until all of the liquid is absorbed. Do not overbeat.

3

Cook the pancakes over medium heat in a cast-iron skillet. Watch carefully because the soy protein isolate causes the batter to brown quickly. Flip and cook until golden brown.

Per pancake: Calories 178, Total Protein 6 g, Soy Protein 4 g, Fat 3 g, Carbohydrates 31 g, Calcium 56 mg, Fiber 2 g, Sodium 137 mg

Creamy Country Gravy

A thick, savory, creamy gravy for biscuits, potatoes, or whatever else you might want to serve with gravy. You can make a thinner gravy by adding a little more water. Use only unflavored soymilk to make this gravy. Using the microwave method eliminates the need for oil in the gravy.

Yield: about 4½ cups

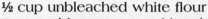

Soymilk

1

Stovetop Method: Toast the flour and nutritional yeast in the oil until it starts to brown. Whip in the soymilk, leaving no lumps. Whip in the tamari, poultry seasoning, onion powder, garlic powder, and black pepper. Heat until it thickens and just starts to boil.

2

Microwave Method: In a 2-quart glass measuring cup, whip together all the ingredients (leaving out the oil if you like). Microwave on high for 4 minutes. Whip until smooth and microwave on high for 4 more minutes. Whip and serve.

½ cup unbleached white flour
2 to 4 tablespoons nutritional yeast flakes
2 tablespoons canola or soy oil
4 cups soymilk, or 2 cups soymilk and 2 cups water or vegetable stock
1 tablespoon tamari
3 teaspoons poultry seasoning
2 teaspoons onion powder
½ teaspoon garlic powder
½ teaspoon freshly ground black pepper

Per ½ cup: Calories 94, Total Protein 5 g, Soy Protein 3 g, Fat 5 g, Carbohydrates 8 g, Calcium 22 mg, Fiber 2 g, Sodium 128 mg

Eggless French Toast

Serve this low-fat, cholesterol-free French toast with syrup, honey, or jelly and a side of Tempeh Breakfast Sausage (page 43).

Yield: 4 to 6 pieces

Tofu

1 (12.3-ounce) package soft silken tofu
¼ cup soymilk or water
2 tablespoons honey or maple syrup
2 tablespoons nutritional yeast flakes (optional)
½ teaspoon cinnamon (optional)
½ teaspoon salt

4 to 6 slices whole grain bread

1

Mix all the ingredients, except the bread, with an electric mixer, a whisk, or in a blender.

2

Dip each slice of bread into the tofu mixture until coated. Brown on each side, either in a nonstick pan or on a lightly oiled griddle. Serve hot.

Per piece: Calories 112, Total Protein 5 g, Soy Protein 3 g, Fat 2 g, Carbohydrates 16 g, Calcium 15 mg, Fiber 3 g, Sodium 319 mg

Mushroom Scrambled Tofu

Yield: 3 cups

Tofu

1

Sauté the tofu, mushrooms, onions, and garlic in the oil.

2

When the tofu starts to brown, stir in the tamari and parsley. Serve with rice, noodles, or toast.

Variation: Omit the mushrooms and add ½ cup chopped green bell pepper and 2 tablespoons nutritional yeast flakes.

1 pound firm tofu, crumbled
1 cup sliced mushrooms
½ cup chopped onions,
    or 1 tablespoon onion powder
1 clove garlic, minced,
    or ¼ teaspoon garlic powder
1 tablespoon oil

1 tablespoon tamari
1 tablespoon chopped fresh
    parsley

Per cup: Calories 214, Total Protein 12 g, Soy Protein 11 g, Fat 16 g, Carbohydrates 6 g, Calcium 170 mg, Fiber 1 g, Sodium 348 mg

Sausage-Flavored Soy Protein

Add this flavorful mixture to Creamy Country Gravy (page 37), or use it as a pizza topping or filling.

Yield: 1½ cups

Textured Soy

⅞ cup boiling water
1 tablespoon tamari
1 cup textured soy protein granules
1 teaspoon onion powder
1 teaspoon sage
½ teaspoon thyme
¼ teaspoon garlic powder
⅛ teaspoon freshly ground black pepper
⅛ teaspoon crushed red pepper
1 tablespoon olive oil

1

Mix the boiling water and tamari together in a bowl. Stir in the textured soy protein, cover, and let stand for about 10 minutes.

2

Fluff the hydrated textured soy protein, and mix in all the flavorings. Sauté in the olive oil over medium heat until browned.

Per ¼ cup: Calories 65, Total Protein 7 g, Soy Protein 7 g, Fat 2 g, Carbohydrates 4 g, Calcium 34 mg, Fiber 1 g, Sodium 171 mg

Scrambled Yuba

Here's another alternative to eggs. Fresh or frozen yuba has the best flavor (page 152).

Yield: 4 servings (3 cups)

Yuba

1

Boil the dried bean curd sticks in water for 20 minutes until soft, or thaw the frozen bean curd sheets.

2

Sauté the onions and garlic in the oil until transparent, then add the rest of the ingredients, and heat through. Serve as you would scrambled eggs, with toast or warm tortillas.

6 ounces dried bean curd sticks, or 3 (8-ounce packages) frozen bean curd sheets

½ cup chopped onions, or 1 tablespoon onion powder

2 cloves garlic, minced, or ½ teaspoon garlic powder

½ tablespoon soy or olive oil

2 tablespoons nutritional yeast flakes

1 tablespoon tamari

½ teaspoon oregano

⅛ teaspoon freshly ground black pepper

Per serving: Calories 232, Total Protein 21 g, Soy Protein 19 g, Fat 11 g, Carbohydrates 11 g, Calcium 98 mg, Fiber 0 g, Sodium 280 mg

Soy Waffles or Pancakes

You can freeze any leftover waffles or pancakes, and reheat them later in the toaster or microwave for a quick meal.

Yield: six 4-inch waffles or twelve 4-inch pancakes

Soy Flour

½ cup unbleached white flour
½ cup whole wheat pastry flour
½ cup cornmeal
½ cup soy flour
¼ cup wheat germ
1 tablespoon baking powder
½ teaspoon salt

2½ cups soymilk, or ¼ cup soymilk powder and 2½ cups water

1

Preheat a nonstick waffle iron or pancake griddle.

2

Mix all the ingredients together, except for the soymilk, and make a well in the middle. Pour in the soymilk and combine until the dry ingredients are just moistened.

3

Lightly oil the waffle iron or griddle, or spray with nonstick cooking spray. Pour the batter onto the preheated waffle iron or pancake griddle, and bake until golden brown. Use about ¼ cup batter per pancake or ⅓ cup per waffle.

4

Flip the pancakes over when they start to bubble up, and brown the other side. Serve with syrup or jelly and Tempeh Breakfast Sausage, (page 43).

Per waffle: Calories 201, Total Protein 11 g, Soy Protein 6 g, Fat 4 g, Carbohydrates 30 g, Calcium 41 mg, Fiber 5 g, Sodium 191 mg

Tempeh Breakfast Sausage

Yield: 6 servings

Tempeh

1

Steam the tempeh for 10 minutes; then cool and grate on the coarse side of a grater.

2

Combine the tempeh with the rest of the ingredients, mix well, and shape into 6 flat cakes, pressing together firmly. (Add a little flour if the mixture is too moist.)

3

Fry in a hot skillet until browned in just enough oil to keep the patties from sticking to the pan.

4

Drain on a paper towel. The patties can be made ahead and frozen. Separate each patty with waxed paper before placing in the freezer.

½ pound fresh or thawed, frozen tempeh

⅓ cup water

2 tablespoons whole wheat pastry flour

1 tablespoon oil

1 tablespoon dark miso

½ teaspoon sage

½ teaspoon thyme

¼ teaspoon marjoram

¼ teaspoon garlic powder

¼ teaspoon cayenne

Per serving: Calories 110, Total Protein 7 g, Soy Protein 7 g, Fat 5 g, Carbohydrates 9 g, Calcium 37 mg, Fiber 3 g, Sodium 2 mg

Tofu Rancheros

Yield: 3½ cups

Tofu

2 tablespoons oil
1 small onion, chopped
1 pound firm tofu, crumbled
1 clove garlic, minced,
    or ½ teaspoon garlic powder

1 large tomato, chopped
2 tablespoons chopped parsley
1 (4-ounce) can green chilies,
    drained and chopped

1

Heat the oil in a skillet, add the onion, tofu, and garlic, and cook for 5 minutes over medium heat.

2

Add the rest of the ingredients, and cook until the tofu starts to turn brown. Serve hot with corn tortillas. Pass the salsa!

Per cup: Calories 206, Total Protein 10 g, Soy Protein 9 g, Fat 13 g, Carbohydrates 10 g, Calcium 158 mg, Fiber 2 g, Sodium 19 mg

Bread

Banana Muffins

Yield: 12 muffins

Soy
Isolate

3 ripe bananas
¼ cup oil
½ cup honey
¼ cup soymilk
1 tablespoon molasses

Dry Ingredients:
2 cups unbleached white flour
½ cup soy protein isolate
1 teaspoon baking powder
1 teaspoon baking soda
½ teaspoon salt
½ cup chopped walnuts (optional)

1

Preheat the oven to 350°F.

2

In a medium mixing bowl, mash the bananas and combine with the oil, honey, soymilk, and molasses.

3

Add the dry ingredients to the liquid mixture, and stir well. Spoon into lightly oiled muffin tins, and bake for 15 to 18 minutes.

Per muffin: Calories 198, Total Protein 6 g, Soy Protein 3 g, Fat 5 g, Carbohydrates 32 g, Calcium 42 mg, Fiber 1 g, Sodium 137 mg

Carrot Raisin Muffins

Yield: 12 muffins

Soy
Isolate

1

Preheat the oven to 350°F.

2

In a medium mixing bowl, mix the carrots with the oil, orange juice, brown sugar, and molasses.

3

Sift the dry ingredients into the carrot mixture, and stir well until all the dry ingredients are absorbed.

4

Add the raisins and stir until they are well distributed in the batter. Evenly fill lightly oiled muffin tins, and bake for 18 to 20 minutes.

1¾ cups grated carrots
¼ cup canola oil
1 cup orange juice
½ cup brown sugar
2 tablespoons molasses

Dry ingredients:
2 cups unbleached white flour
⅔ cup soy protein isolate
1 teaspoon cinnamon
1 teaspoon baking soda
1 teaspoon baking powder
½ teaspoon salt

1 cup raisins

Per muffin: Calories 211, Total Protein 7 g, Soy Protein 4 g, Fat 5 g, Carbohydrates 36 g, Calcium 57 mg, Fiber 2 g, Sodium 163 mg

Dinner Rolls

Soymilk

Yield: 12 rolls

Sponge:
3 tablespoons honey
1 cup water
1 cup soymilk
1½ cups unbleached flour
1 package baking yeast
   (2½ teaspoons)

½ teaspoon salt
2 tablespoons sesame seeds
2 tablespoons canola oil
¾ cup soy protein isolate
½ cup cooked oatmeal (optional)
1 cup whole wheat flour
1½ cups unbleached white flour

1

In a mixing bowl, beat together the honey, water, soymilk, flour, and yeast until a smooth, thick sponge is formed. Let set for 10 to 15 minutes. You should see bubbles forming in the batter.

2

Mix the remaining ingredients into the bowl of bubbling sponge until everything is well blended and smooth. Turn out onto a clean counter to knead. Knead until a satiny dough is formed, about 5 to 10 minutes.

3

Lightly oil the sides of the mixing bowl, and put the kneaded dough back into the bowl. Lightly oil the top of the dough, and let it rise until doubled.

4

After the dough has risen, preheat the oven to 350°F. Break the dough into twelve equal pieces, and roll them into 2-inch balls. Place the balls on a cookie sheet, and let them rise again for 15 to 20 minutes.

5

Place the balls in the hot oven, and bake for 15 to 20 minutes until golden brown.

Per roll: Calories 208, Total Protein 10 g, Soy Protein 5 g, Fat 4 g, Carbohydrates 33 g, Calcium 74 mg, Fiber 3 g, Sodium 160 mg

Eggless Blueberry Soy Muffins

Make these sweet, hearty muffins with either fresh or frozen blueberries. These muffins freeze well.

Yield: 12 muffins

Soymilk

1

Preheat the oven to 400°F.

2

Mix the dry ingredients together, and make a well in the middle.

3

Whip together the soymilk, honey, oil, and vanilla, and pour into the well in the dry ingredients. Stir just until blended.

4

Fold in the blueberries, pour into oiled muffin tins, and bake for about 20 minutes until browned.

Dry Ingredients:
¾ cup unbleached white flour
¾ cup whole wheat pastry flour
½ cup soy flour
¼ cup wheat germ
3 teaspoons baking powder
½ teaspoon salt

1½ cups soymilk or soy yogurt (page 30)
½ cup honey
2 tablespoons canola oil
1 teaspoon vanilla

1 cup fresh or frozen blueberries

Per muffin: Calories 160, Total Protein 5 g, Soy Protein 3 g, Fat 4 g, Carbohydrates 26 g, Calcium 25 mg, Fiber 3 g, Sodium 95 mg

Light, High-Protein Wheat-Soy Bread

Use this light bread with a sweet, nutty flavor to make sandwiches, toast, or just eat it by the slice.

Yield: 2 loaves or 16 buns

Soymilk

3 cups soymilk
2 tablespoons sweetener of your choice
1 tablespoon baking yeast
2 teaspoons salt
4 cups unbleached white flour
2 cups soy flour
3 to 4 cups whole wheat flour

1

Scald the soymilk, dissolve the sweetener in it, and cool to lukewarm. Sprinkle the baking yeast over the top, and let stand until the yeast starts foaming.

2

Stir in the salt and flour, and beat until smooth. Beat in the soy flour until smooth. Add enough whole wheat flour to make a firm dough, and knead until smooth. Cover and let rise until almost double in bulk.

3

Punch down the dough and form into 2 loaves or 16 buns. Let rise again until almost double in bulk.

4

Preheat the oven to 350°F. Bake the loaves for about 45 minutes or the buns for about 20 minutes. Brush the tops with soy oil.

Per bun: Calories 273, Total Protein 13 g, Soy Protein 6 g, Fat 5 g, Carbohydrates 46 g, Calcium 83 mg, Fiber 6 g, Sodium 274 mg

Peach Bread

Yield: 8 to 10 slices

Soy Isolate

1

Preheat the oven to 350°F.

2

In a medium mixing bowl, combine the oil, sugars, vanilla, orange juice, and peaches.

3

Sift the flour, soy protein isolate, salt, baking powder, and baking soda into liquid mixture. Stir well until all the dry ingredients are absorbed.

4

Spoon the batter into a lightly oiled bread pan, and bake for 40 to 45 minutes.

⅓ cup canola oil
½ cup brown sugar
½ cup white sugar
1 teaspoon vanilla
½ cup orange juice
2 cups chopped peaches

2 cups unbleached white flour
½ cup soy protein isolate
½ teaspoon salt
1 teaspoon baking powder
1 teaspoon baking soda

Per slice: Calories 267, Total Protein 7 g, Soy Protein 4 g, Fat 7 g, Carbohydrates 42 g, Calcium 86 mg, Fiber 1 g, Sodium 319 mg

Multi-Grain Potato Soy Bread

Vary the flavor of this high-protein, multi-grain bread with whatever grains and flours you have on hand.

Yield: 2 loves or 16 buns

Soy Flour

4 tablespoons sweetener of your choice
3 cups lukewarm potato cooking water
¼ cup soy oil
1 tablespoon baking yeast

2 teaspoons salt
3 cups unbleached white flour
½ cup rolled oats
½ cup quinoa
½ cup brown rice or barley flour
½ cup soy flour
3 cups whole wheat flour or spelt flour
2 teaspoons salt

1

Dissolve the sweetener in the potato water, and mix in the oil. Sprinkle the baking yeast over the top, and let stand until the yeast starts foaming.

2

Stir in the salt and unbleached flour, and beat until smooth. Beat in the rolled oats, quinoa, brown rice flour, and soy flour until smooth. Add the whole wheat four, and beat and knead until smooth. Cover and let rise until almost double in bulk.

3

Preheat the oven to 350°F. Punch down the dough and form into 2 loaves or 16 buns. Let rise again until almost double in bulk. Bake the loaves for about 45 minutes or the buns for about 20 minutes. Brush the tops with oil.

Per bun: Calories 260, Total Protein 8 g, Soy Protein 1 g, Fat 5 g, Carbohydrates 45 g, Calcium 58 mg, Fiber 5 g, Sodium 270 mg

Salads &
Dressings

Asian Greek Salad

This salad combines Asian, Greek, and south of the border flavors. This recipe is adapted from the Greek Salad in *Tofu Cookery*.

Yield: 6 to 8 servings

Tofu

¼ cup olive oil
2 tablespoons wine vinegar
2 tablespoons miso
¼ teaspoon freshly ground black
   pepper
2 cloves garlic
2 tablespoons chopped fresh
   basil
1 tablespoon chopped fresh
   oregano
1 pound firm tofu, cut in ½-inch
   cubes
1 head leaf lettuce
2 fresh tomatoes, cubed
2 cucumbers, cubed
1 avocado, cubed
½ small red onion, chopped
½ cup Greek or black olives

1

Blend the olive oil, vinegar, miso, black pepper, and garlic. Stir in the basil and oregano.

2

Pour the dressing over the tofu cubes in a glass or stainless steel bowl, and marinate at least 1 hour or overnight.

3

Wash and dry the lettuce, and arrange in a salad bowl. Toss the marinated tofu and all the rest of the ingredients together, and serve in the lettuce-lined bowl.

Per serving: Calories 219, Total Protein 6 g, Soy Protein 5 g, Fat 16 g, Carbohydrates 12 g, Calcium 113 mg, Fiber 4 g, Sodium 85 mg

Bangkok Cold Noodle Salad

An Indonesian favorite that makes a complete luncheon.

Yield: 6 servings

1

Simmer the tempeh in the vegetable stock and tamari for 25 minutes in a covered pan. Drain and cut the tempeh into small dice.

2

Mix the marinade ingredients and marinate the tempeh for at least 2 hours. Cook the Chinese noodles for 2 minutes in boiling water. Drain, run cold water over the noodles to cool, and drain again.

3

Roast the prepared vegetables for 10 minutes at 350°F.

4

Toss together the roasted vegetables, noodles, tempeh, and marinade. Sprinkle with the toasted sesame seeds. Keep chilled if made ahead.

*If fresh noodles are not available in your produce section, you can substitute ¾ pound of linguine. Cook the pasta 7 to 8 minutes until tender, but firm; drain, rinse in cold water, and drain again.

½ pound tempeh
1 cup vegetable stock
1 tablespoon tamari

Marinade:
2 tablespoons lemon juice
2 tablespoons mirin
2 tablespoons tamari
1 tablespoon dark sesame oil
2 teaspoons grated gingerroot

1 (14-ounce package) fresh Chinese noodles, cut in 3-inch lengths*

1 cup thinly sliced green onions
1 medium carrot, grated
1 cup finely diced celery (Use a vegetable peeler to remove strings from the ribs of celery before slicing.)

⅓ cup sesame seeds, toasted

Per serving: Calories 346, Total Protein 12 g, Soy Protein 3 g, Fat 7 g, Carbohydrates 57 g, Calcium 115 mg, Fiber 3 g, Sodium 526 mg

Mock Chicken Salad

Yield: 4 cups

Tofu

1 pound firm tofu, cut in ½-inch
  cubes
2 tablespoons fresh lemon juice
½ teaspoon celery salt

1 cup diced celery
¼ cup minced green onions
½ cup slivered, toasted almonds
½ teaspoon salt

1 cup Mock Sour Cream Dressing
  (page 34)

1
Combine the tofu, lemon juice, and celery salt in a bowl. Add the rest of the ingredients, mix well, chill, and serve.

Per ½ cup: Calories 173, Total Protein 8 g, Soy Protein 6 g, Fat 13 g, Carbohydrates 6 g,
Calcium 125 mg, Fiber 2 g, Sodium 314 mg

Sweet Bean Salad

Yield: 4 to 6 servings

1

Thaw and rinse the frozen green soybeans. Mix the vegetables in a bowl.

2

Thoroughly mix the dressing, then toss with the vegetable mixture. Serve cold.

1 (16-ounce) package frozen
  green soybeans
½ cup chopped onions
½ cup chopped celery
½ cup chopped red pepper

Dressing:
½ cup vegetable oil
½ cup white vinegar
½ cup sugar

Per serving: Calories 403, Total Protein 12 g, Soy Protein 11 g, Fat 24 g, Carbohydrates 30 g,
Calcium 141 mg, Fiber 2 g, Sodium 13 mg

Thai Noodle Salad

Add fresh hot pepper to this salad to make it as fiery as you like.

Yield: 8 to 9 cups

Tempeh

½ pound tempeh

½ pound soba or angel hair
noodles

2 tablespoons water
1 tablespoon lime juice or rice
vinegar
1 tablespoon tamari
2 teaspoons grated gingerroot
⅛ teaspoon cracked red pepper
or hot pepper of choice
½ tablespoon soy or peanut oil
2 cups grated carrots
1 cup thinly sliced celery
½ cup chopped fresh cilantro
½ cup chopped green onions
¼ cup chopped peanuts
2 tablespoons lime juice
2 tablespoons sweetener of
choice
1 tablespoon tamari
2 teaspoons toasted sesame or
peanut oil
1 teaspoon grated gingerroot
1 clove garlic, minced

1

Steam the tempeh for 20 minutes. Cut into ¼ x ½-inch pieces.

2

Cook the pasta in boiling water until tender, then rinse and drain.

3

Mix together the water, 1 tablespoon lime juice, 1 tablespoon tamari, 2 teaspoons gingerroot, and red pepper. Pour over the tempeh pieces, and toss to distribute the sauce evenly. Brown in a nonstick skillet with the ½ tablespoon oil.

4

In a salad bowl, mix together the carrots, celery, cilantro, green onions, peanuts, 2 tablespoons lime juice, sweetener, 1 tablespoon tamari, 2 teaspoons oil, 1 teaspoon gingerroot, and 1 clove garlic. Add the browned tempeh and the pasta, toss, and serve.

Per cup: Calories 206, Total Protein 10 g, Soy Protein 5 g, Fat 6 g, Carbohydrates 27 g,
Calcium 61 mg, Fiber 3 g, Sodium 279 mg

Tofu No-Egg Salad

Serve as a sandwich spread or as an appetizer on crackers.

Yield: 3 to 4 servings

1

Combine all the ingredients, except the tofu, in a bowl or pint jar, and mix well.

2

Crumble the tofu in a bowl, and pour the dressing over. Mash together with a fork.

⅓ cup olive oil
¼ cup apple cider vinegar
1 teaspoon tamari
2 tablespoons honey
1 tablespoon pickle relish
1½ teaspoons celery seed
1 teaspoon salt
Pinch cayenne
½ teaspoon dill weed
½ teaspoon turmeric powder
¼ teaspoon garlic powder
¼ teaspoon paprika
¼ teaspoon black pepper

1 pound firm tofu

Per serving: Calories 317, Total Protein 9 g, Soy Protein 9 g, Fat 23 g, Carbohydrates 15 g, Calcium 143 mg, Fiber 1 g, Sodium 745 mg

Tofu Vegetable Salad

This versatile salad can make a sandwich, stuff a pita, top a bed of lettuce, or serve as a dip or spread with vegetables, chips, or crackers.

Yield: 4 servings (about 3 cups)

½ pound soft silken tofu
3 tablespoons apple cider vinegar
1½ tablespoons sweetener of choice
1 teaspoon onion powder
1 teaspoon turmeric
½ teaspoon salt
½ teaspoon garlic powder

½ pound firm tofu
½ cup chopped celery
½ cup finely grated carrots (optional)
½ cup chopped cucumbers (optional)
¼ cup chopped onions
¼ cup chopped parsley

1

In a blender or food processor, blend the soft tofu, vinegar, sweetener, onion powder, turmeric, salt, and garlic powder until smooth.

2

Crumble the firm tofu into a bowl. Mix in the celery, carrot, cucumber, onion, and parsley. Stir in the blended tofu mixture, and serve.

Per serving: Calories 108, Total Protein 7 g, Soy Protein 7 g, Fat 4 g, Carbohydrates 11 g, Calcium 89 mg, Fiber 1 g, Sodium 294 mg

Wild Rice Salad

Yield: 6 servings

1

Add the rice to a large pot of boiling water. Simmer for 30 to 35 minutes, or until the rice is tender. Rinse under cold running water, and drain.

2

To prepare the dressing, whisk the oil, vinegar, juice, honey, orange rind, and salt in a bowl.

3

Add the rice mixture, green soybeans, celery, apple, and dates. Refrigerate for at least 2 hours or overnight. Serve cold.

½ cup brown rice
½ cup wild rice

Dressing:
½ cup olive oil
⅓ cup red wine vinegar
½ cup orange juice
2 teaspoons honey
1 tablespoon grated orange rind
1 teaspoon salt

½ cup green vegetable soybeans, cooked, cooled, and drained
2 tablespoons chopped celery
2 tablespoons chopped apple
1 cup chopped dates

Per serving: Calories 399, Total Protein 5 g, Soy Protein 2 g, Fat 18 g, Carbohydrates 52 g, Calcium 51 mg, Fiber 5 g, Sodium 420 mg

Creamy Cilantro Tofu

Serve this in place of sour cream for any Mexican entrée or as an appetizer with chips or raw vegetables.

Yield: 1¼ cups

Tofu

1 large clove garlic
1 small jalapeño (optional),
   or ⅛ teaspoon dried hot pepper
1 cup fresh cilantro leaves

1½ cups soft silken tofu, or ½
   pound regular tofu and 6
   tablespoons water
1 tablespoon lime juice
½ teaspoon salt

1

Chop the garlic in a food processor. Add the jalapeño and chop, then add the cilantro leaves and chop. Remove from the food processor, and set aside.

2

Add the tofu, lime juice, and salt to the processor, and process until smooth and creamy. Fold in the garlic, cilantro, and jalapeño. Serve chilled.

Creamy Cumin Tofu: Substitute 1 teaspoon cumin powder for the cilantro.

Per 2 tablespoons: Calories 14, Total Protein 2 g, Soy Protein 2 g, Fat 0 g, Carbohydrates 1 g, Calcium 3 mg, Fiber 0 g, Sodium 160 mg

Green Goddess Dressing

A San Francisco favorite with salad greens and avocado.

Yield: 1¾ cups

Tofu

1

Combine all the ingredients in a blender, and blend until smooth and creamy.

½ pound soft silken tofu, mashed
2 tablespoons oil
2 tablespoons vinegar
½ tablespoon dry chives
¼ cup fresh parsley
1 teaspoon onion powder
½ teaspoon salt
¼ teaspoon garlic powder
⅛ teaspoon black pepper

Per 2 tablespoons: Calories 29, Total Protein 1 g, Soy Protein 1 g, Fat 2 g, Carbohydrates 0 g, Calcium 18 mg, Fiber 0 g, Sodium 77 mg

Miso-Ginger Sauce

Use this easy-to-make, zippy sauce as a salad dressing or sauce for steamed vegetables.

Yield: ½ cup

Miso

1

Combine all the ingredients in a blender until smooth and creamy.

⅓ cup sweet yellow miso
1½ tablespoons lemon juice or rice vinegar
2 tablespoons honey
1 clove garlic, pressed
1 teaspoon gingerroot, grated

Per 2 tablespoons: Calories 82, Total Protein 2 g, Soy Protein 2 g, Fat 1 g, Carbohydrates 15 g, Calcium 17 mg, Fiber 1 g, Sodium 1 mg

Miso Honey Mustard Dressing or Dip

Serve with salad as a dressing or as a dip with raw vegetables.

Yield: ¾ cup

Miso

¼ cup sweet yellow miso
¼ cup rice vinegar
2 tablespoons soy oil
1 tablespoon honey
¼ teaspoon dry mustard

1

Combine all the ingredients in a blender until smooth and creamy.

Per 2 tablespoons: Calories 76, Total Protein 1 g, Soy Protein 1 g, Fat 5 g, Carbohydrates 7 g, Calcium 8 mg, Fiber 1 g, Sodium 0 mg

Miso Salad Dressing or Sauce

This recipe calls for sweet yellow miso, but you can substitute a darker miso if you like. The flavor will change subtly by using a different miso.

Yield: 1 cup

Miso

1 tablespoon sesame oil
6 tablespoons sweet yellow miso
6 tablespoons water
2 tablespoons rice vinegar
1 tablespoon honey
2 teaspoons grated onion,
   or 1 teaspoon onion powder

1

Combine all the ingredients in a blender until smooth and creamy.

2

To serve hot, heat, but do not boil. Serve over steamed vegetables, grains, or tofu.

Per 2 tablespoons: Calories 50, Total Protein 1 g, Soy Protein 1 g, Fat 2 g, Carbohydrates 6 g, Calcium 9 mg, Fiber 1 g, Sodium 0 mg

Sweet Sesame Dressing

This dressing is delicious with cold cooked grains.

Yield: 1 cup

Miso

1

Combine all the ingredients in a blender or food processor, and blend until creamy smooth.

½ cup sesame tahini
½ cup water
2 teaspoons lemon juice
2 teaspoons light miso
2 teaspoons rice syrup or honey

Per 2 tablespoons: Calories 31, Total Protein 2 g, Soy Protein 1 g, Fat 2 g, Carbohydrates 1 g, Calcium 31 mg, Fiber 0 g, Sodium 87 mg

Tahini Tofu Dressing

Yield: 1½ cups

Tofu

1

Combine all the ingredients in a blender or food processor, and blend until creamy smooth. Chill for use on salad or fruit dishes.

½ pound soft silken tofu
3 tablespoons lemon juice
2 tablespoons tahini
2 tablespoons water
1 tablespoon tamari
1 tablespoon mirin

Per 2 tablespoons: Calories 31, Total Protein 2 g, Soy Protein 1 g, Fat 2 g, Carbohydrates 1 g, Calcium 31 mg, Fiber 0 g, Sodium 87 mg

Tartar Sauce

Serve Tartar Sauce with Soy Fish Cakes (page 92) or Baked Tofu Nuggets (page 33).

Yield: 1¾ cups

Tofu

1¼ cups soft silken tofu
2 tablespoons lemon juice
2 teaspoons onion powder
½ teaspoon dry mustard
½ teaspoon salt

6 tablespoons chopped onion
3 tablespoons sweet pickle relish

1
Combine the tofu, lemon juice, onion powder, mustard, and salt in a blender until smooth and creamy.

2
Fold in the onion and pickle relish.

Thousand Island Dressing: Add ¼ cup ketchup when blending the ingredients together.

Per 2 tablespoons: Calories 15, Total Protein 2 g, Soy Protein 2 g, Fat 0 g, Carbohydrates 2 g, Calcium 2 mg, Fiber 0 g, Sodium 118 mg

Soups &
Sandwiches

Corn Chowder

Yield: 2 quarts

Tofu

2 onions, chopped
1 red or green bell pepper, chopped
2 ribs celery, chopped
2 small potatoes, cut in ½-inch cubes
2 cloves garlic, pressed
2 tablespoons oil
4 cups water
1 small bay leaf
¼ teaspoon thyme

4 teaspoons vegetable bouillon powder
2½ cups frozen corn
½ pound firm tofu, cut in ¼-inch cubes
¼ teaspoon freshly ground black pepper

1

Sauté the onions, pepper, celery, potatoes, and garlic in the oil until the onions are transparent.

2

Add the water, bay leaf, and thyme. Bring the soup to a boil and cook until the vegetables are almost tender.

3

Add the bouillon powder, corn, tofu, and black pepper. Serve when the corn is tender. Garnish with red and green bell pepper rings.

Per cup: Calories 141, Total Protein 4 g, Soy Protein 2 g, Fat 4 g, Carbohydrates 21 g, Calcium 49 mg, Fiber 4 g, Sodium 17 mg

French Miso Onion Soup

Miso

1

Heat the oil in a heavy pan, add the onions, and cook very slowly for 1 hour, stirring often.

2

Add the 3 cups vegetable stock and bring to a boil. Simmer for 5 minutes.

3

Dissolve the miso in the ½ cup warm water. Stir the miso mixture into the soup, and cook 5 more minutes; do not boil. Serve with whole wheat croutons, and soy Parmesan cheese.

2 tablespoons plain or dark sesame oil
8 medium onions, thinly sliced

3 cups vegetable stock or warm water
2 tablespoons dark barley or brown rice miso
2 tablespoons light miso
½ cup warm water or vegetable stock

Per serving: Calories 137, Total Protein 3 g, Soy Protein 1 g, Fat 6 g, Carbohydrates 16 g, Calcium 45 mg, Fiber 2 g, Sodium 180 mg

Miso-Tofu Soup

You can try different flavors of miso to vary the taste of this soup.

Yield: 6 to 8 servings

Miso

6 cups water
1 carrot, cut in matchstick size
    pieces
1 small onion, cut in rounds
½ pound watercress, coarsely
    chopped
½ pound regular tofu,
    or ½ package firm silken tofu,
    cut in small cubes
½ cup sweet white miso

1

Bring the water to a boil, and add the carrot. Turn off the heat and add the onion, watercress, and tofu.

2

Dip out ½ cup hot water from the pot, and mix together with the miso.

3

Continue stirring until the mixture is smooth, then pour it back into the soup pot, and stir. Do not boil. Serve immediately.

Per serving: Calories 79, Total Protein 5 g, Soy Protein 4 g, Fat 2 g, Carbohydrates 9 g, Calcium 92 mg, Fiber 2 g, Sodium 20 mg

Southwestern Chili

This chili is easy to put together and showcases the chewy texture of frozen tofu.

Yield: 7 cups

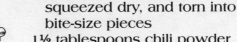

Tofu

1

In a 3-quart soup pot, sauté the green pepper, onion, and garlic in the oil.

2

When they are almost tender, add the tofu, chili powder, cumin, and salt. Continue to cook until the vegetables are tender, then add the beans and water. Heat until hot and serve.

1 medium green pepper, diced
1 medium onion, diced
2 cloves garlic, minced
2 tablespoons oil

1 pound firm tofu, frozen, thawed, squeezed dry, and torn into bite-size pieces
1½ tablespoons chili powder
1 teaspoon cumin
1 teaspoon salt

1 (30-ounce) can pinto or kidney beans, drained
3 cups water

Per cup: Calories 262, Total Protein 13 g, Soy Protein 5 g, Fat 7 g, Carbohydrates 35 g, Calcium 136 mg, Fiber 7 g, Sodium 312 mg

Soy Minestrone

Yield: 8 to 10 servings

2 cups celery with leaves
1 six-inch leek (white bulb only)
½ cup chopped yellow onions
4 carrots, cut in quarters
1½ cups frozen green vegetable
    soybeans
4 to 5 cloves garlic
⅓ cup olive oil

1 (28-ounce) can tomatoes with
    juice
6 cups water
2 tablespoons miso
½ cup white wine
1½ cups uncooked macaroni
1 teaspoon salt
1 teaspoon thyme
½ teaspoon oregano
½ teaspoon dried basil

1

Chop the celery, leek, onion, carrots, and garlic in a food processor. Sauté the chopped vegetables and frozen soybeans in the olive oil in a Dutch oven for 10 minutes.

2

Purée the tomatoes with their juice in a food processor or blender, and add to the vegetables.

3

Add the water, miso, wine, macaroni, and seasonings. Simmer for 10 to 15 minutes.

Variations: You can add thinly sliced zucchini for the last 10 minutes of the cooking time.

You can also add 1 drained (14-ounce) can garbanzo beans, and 1 (10-ounce) package frozen corn.

Per serving: Calories 259, Total Protein 9 g, Soy Protein 4 g, Fat 9 g, Carbohydrates 31 g, Calcium 101 mg, Fiber 7 g, Sodium 288 mg

"Beef"-Style Veggie Burgers

This recipe can easily be doubled to make a dozen burgers.

Yield: 6 burgers

Textured Soy

1

Combine the textured soy protein, hot water, ketchup, salt, oregano, marjoram, and garlic in a medium sized bowl. Let stand 10 minutes, then mix with the carrots, celery, onion, and parsley.

2

Stir in the gluten flour to make a firm mixture. (Instant gluten flour will give you a chewier burger, but regular wheat flour will work fine.)

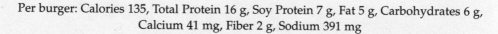

3

Press the mixture firmly into 6 flat patties, about 4 inches wide, using about ½ cup of the mixture for each patty. Heat a skillet and add the oil. Fry the patties for 8 to 10 minutes on each side over medium-low heat until browned. Serve in buns.

1 cup textured soy protein granules
¾ cup hot water
1 tablespoon ketchup
1 teaspoon salt
½ teaspoon oregano
½ teaspoon marjoram
½ teaspoon garlic powder

¼ cup grated carrots
¼ cup finely chopped celery
2 tablespoons finely chopped green onions
2 tablespoons finely chopped fresh parsley

½ cup instant gluten flour, or ¼ cup unbleached white or whole wheat flour

2 tablespoons oil

Per burger: Calories 135, Total Protein 16 g, Soy Protein 7 g, Fat 5 g, Carbohydrates 6 g, Calcium 41 mg, Fiber 2 g, Sodium 391 mg

High-Protein Burgers

Yield: 6 burgers

Textured
Soy

¾ cup boiling water
2 tablespoons tamari
1 cup textured soy protein
    granules

¼ cup chopped onions
¼ cup chopped green pepper
1 clove garlic, minced

½ pound firm tofu, mashed
¼ cup ketchup
1 tablespoon Dijon mustard
¼ teaspoon freshly ground black
    pepper
½ cup whole wheat flour

1 tablespoon olive oil

1

Mix together the boiling water and tamari. Pour over the textured soy protein granules, cover, and let stand for about 10 minutes.

2

Mix the onions, green pepper, and garlic in a microwave-safe bowl, cover, and microwave on high for 1 minute. As an alternative, you can simmer these in ¼ cup water for 3 minutes.

3

Mix all the ingredients, except the olive oil, and form into 6 burgers. Oil a nonstick griddle with the olive oil, and brown the burgers on both sides. Let the burgers cool a few minutes before serving so they will firm up. Serve on toasted buns with all the fixings.

Per burger: Calories 147, Total Protein 11 g, Soy Protein 10 g, Fat 4 g, Carbohydrates 15 g, Calcium 81 mg, Fiber 3 g, Sodium 516 mg

Pizza Burgers

Yield: 6 burgers

Tempeh

1

Steam the tempeh for 20 minutes, then drain and cool.

2

In a large skillet, braise the onion and pepper in the water until tender, about 8 minutes.

3

Grate the tempeh into the skillet with the onion and pepper. Stir in the tamari and spices, and cook for 5 minutes.

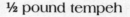

4

Add the tomato paste and cook 5 to 10 more minutes. Serve between English muffins.

½ pound tempeh

1 medium onion, chopped
1 green pepper, chopped
1 to 3 tablespoons water

2 tablespoons tamari
1 teaspoon oregano
1 teaspoon basil
½ teaspoon marjoram
¼ teaspoon red pepper flakes

1 (8-ounce) can tomato paste
6 whole wheat English muffins, split

Per burger: Calories 253, Total Protein 13 g, Soy Protein 7 g, Fat 4 g, Carbohydrates 40 g, Calcium 84 mg, Fiber 6 g, Sodium 563 mg

Powerhouse Sandwich

Yield: 4 sandwiches

Tempeh

½ pound tempeh, sliced in 4
    pieces, or 4 commercial
    tempeh burgers of your choice
8 slices multi-grain bread
3 tablespoons soy mayonnaise
    (about 1 teaspoon per slice)
4 slices soy mozzarella cheese
4 slices tomato
4 cups clover or alfalfa sprouts
4 pieces Romaine lettuce
Herbal seasoning to taste

1

Steam the tempeh for 20 minutes. Coat a large skillet with nonstick cooking spray, and brown the tempeh. (If you are using tempeh burgers, cook according to the package directions.)

2

Spread the bread with the mayonnaise, and top 4 slices with the tempeh, cheese, tomato, sprouts, lettuce, and seasoning. Cover with the remaining slices of bread, slice in half, and serve with crisp dill pickle spears.

Per sandwich: Calories 342, Total Protein 17 g, Soy Protein 12 g, Fat 16 g,
Carbohydrates 31 g, Calcium 72 mg, Fiber 11 g, Sodium 284 mg

Quick & Easy Sloppy Joes

Lunch can be ready in 10 minutes with these.

Yield: 4 servings

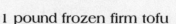

Tofu

1

Defrost and press out the excess liquid from the tofu, and slice it into thin strips and pieces. Add the barbecue sauce, heat, and pile into the buns.

1 pound frozen firm tofu
1 cup barbecue sauce of your choice
4 whole grain burger buns, warmed

Per serving: Calories 280, Total Protein 12 g, Soy Protein 8 g, Fat 5 g, Carbohydrates 44 g, Calcium 177 mg, Fiber 3 g, Sodium 1170 mg

Ruebens en Croissant

A French twist on an old favorite, but traditionalists can use rye bread.

Yield: 6 servings

Tempeh

½ pound tempeh
2 tablespoons oil
1 (16-ounce) can sauerkraut,
    drained

6 croissants, sliced in half
2 ounces soy Swiss cheese,
    sliced
3 tablespoons Thousand Island
    Dressing (page 66)

1

Steam the tempeh for 20 minutes, and cool. Cut the tempeh in half crosswise, making 2 thin slabs. Cut each slab into 3 pieces. Heat a skillet and brown the tempeh slices in the oil. Warm the sauerkraut.

2

On 6 croissant halves, place a slice of tempeh, a spoonful of sauerkraut, a slice of cheese, and ½ tablespoon of dressing. If desired, place under a broiler for a few minutes to melt the cheese before you add the dressing. Top with the remaining half croissant.

Per serving: Calories 412, Total Protein 15 g, Soy Protein 6 g, Fat 22 g, Carbohydrates 38 g, Calcium 170 mg, Fiber 5 g, Sodium 1056 mg

Soy Burgers

Use your leftover cooked soybeans to make these burgers or Soy Non-Meat Balls (see variation below). Serve Soy Burgers on fat-free buns with mustard, lettuce, and tomato. Soy Non-Meat Balls are a great accompaniment to pasta.

Yield: 8 burgers

Soybeans

1

If you don't have leftover soy beans, pressure cook 1 cup unsoaked dried soybeans in 3 cups water for 60 to 75 minutes until they are so soft you can mash one on the roof of your mouth with your tongue. One cup dried beans yields about 2 cups cooked.

2

Drain the soy beans and mash with a potato masher, or chop in a food processor. Stir the mashed beans into the rest of the ingredients, mix well, and form into 8 balls.

3

Flatten each ball to about ½ inch thick or less. Fry in a nonstick skillet sprayed with nonstick cooking spray. Cook until browned on both sides.

Soy Non-Meat Balls: Form into 24 balls. Spray a 9 x 13-inch pan with nonstick cooking spray or spread with 1 tablespoon oil. Arrange the balls evenly in the pan, and bake at 350°F for 30 to 40 minutes, rolling the balls every 10 minutes to brown on all sides.

2 cups cooked soybeans
½ cup uncooked rolled oats or whole wheat flour
½ cup oat bran or wheat germ
½ cup finely chopped onions, or 2 teaspoons onion powder
1 clove garlic, minced, or ½ teaspoon garlic powder
2 tablespoons tomato paste or ketchup
1 teaspoon salt
½ teaspoon oregano
½ teaspoon basil

Per burger: Calories 123, Total Protein 8 g, Soy Protein 6 g, Fat 4 g, Carbohydrates 12 g, Calcium 56 mg, Fiber 4 g, Sodium 270 mg

Tofu Veggie Burgers

Tofu

½ pound firm tofu
¾ cup dry rolled oats

1 small onion, chopped
¼ cup chopped marinated
  roasted red peppers
¼ cup grated carrots
1 tablespoon tamari

1

Preheat the oven to 350°F.

2

Drain and mash the tofu in a medium-sized mixing bowl, mix in the oats, and set aside.

3

Spray a small saucepan with nonstick cooking spray, and sauté the onion for about 3 to 4 minutes until tender. Add to the tofu mix. Add the red peppers, carrots, and tamari, and mix well.

4

Use a ¼ cup measuring cup to measure out each burger. Press and shape with your hands, and place on an oiled cookie sheet.

5

Bake for 15 minutes on one side, flip over, and bake for 10 more minutes.

Per burger: Calories 61, Total Protein 4 g, Soy Protein 2 g, Fat 1 g, Carbohydrates 7 g, Calcium 39 mg, Fiber 1 g, Sodium 129 mg

Main Dishes

Broccoli Cashew Stir-Fry

Yield: 6 servings

1½ cups water
Pinch of sea salt
2 cups sliced carrots
2 cups broccoli florets, cut into 2-
  inch pieces

1 cup cashew pieces

1-inch fresh gingerroot, minced
2 onions, thinly sliced
1 tablespoon sesame oil

1 pound tofu, cut into cubes
Vegetable cooking liquid

2 tablespoons arrowroot
3 tablespoons tamari

1

Bring the water to a boil, add the salt,.carrots, and broccoli, and boil for 1 minute. Drain and reserve the liquid for the sauce.

2

Roast the cashews for 10 minutes at 350°F.

3

Heat a wok or large skillet over medium-high heat, and stir-fry the ginger and onions in the oil for 1 minute.

4

Add the carrots, broccoli, and cashews, and stir-fry 2 more minutes. Gently stir in the tofu and vegetable liquid. Cover the pan and let steam for 1 minute.

5

Mix the arrowroot and tamari together. Push the vegetables to one side of the pan, and add the arrowroot mixture to the juices. Let it boil up, then toss the vegetables gently into the sauce as it thickens. Serve over short or long grain rice or dry Chinese noodles.

Per serving: Calories 287, Total Protein 11 g, Soy Protein 6 g, Fat 16 g, Carbohydrates 23 g, Calcium 136 mg, Fiber 4 g, Sodium 556 mg

Broccoli Quiche

Yield: 6 servings

Tofu

1
Preheat the oven to 350°F.

2
Boil the broccoli in 1 inch of water for 5 minutes, and drain.

3
Sauté the onions and garlic in the oil until soft.

4
Combine half the tofu with the lemon juice, mustard, salt, and black pepper in a food processor or blender until smooth and creamy. Fold in the remaining tofu, onions and garlic, and broccoli. Bake in an oiled 9-inch pie pan for about 30 minutes, and serve hot.

3 cups broccoli florets

1 cup chopped onions
3 cloves garlic, minced
2 tablespoons oil

1 pound regular tofu, crumbled
2 tablespoons lemon juice
1 tablespoon dry mustard
1 teaspoon salt
½ teaspoon black pepper

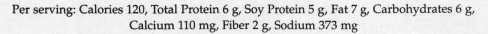
Per serving: Calories 120, Total Protein 6 g, Soy Protein 5 g, Fat 7 g, Carbohydrates 6 g, Calcium 110 mg, Fiber 2 g, Sodium 373 mg

Chinese Foo Yung with Tofu

Yield: 8 servings

Tofu

2 pounds tofu
¼ cup tamari
¾ cup whole wheat flour
2 teaspoons baking powder

1 clove garlic, minced
1 inch gingerroot, minced
1 medium onion, chopped
1 green pepper, chopped
1 cup thinly sliced celery
2 tablespoons light sesame oil
1 teaspoon dark sesame oil
2 cups mung bean sprouts
1 (8-ounce) can water chestnuts,
  chopped

1
Place 1½ pounds of the tofu and the tamari in a food processor or blender, and blend until smooth. (Reserve ½ pound of the tofu, and crumble for step number 2.) Blend in the flour and baking powder.
Heat a skillet and stir-fry the garlic, gingerroot, onion, green pepper, and celery in the two sesame oils over medium-high heat. Stir in the bean sprouts and water chestnuts.

2
Combine the tofu mixture, the vegetables, and the reserved tofu, mixing well.

3
Preheat the oven to 350°F. Form 8 large, round patties, and place 1 inch apart on a lightly oiled cookie sheet. Bake for 20 minutes, turn over, and bake 10 to 15 more minutes. Serve with Mushroom

Mushroom Gravy

1 cup diced mushrooms
1 teaspoon sesame oil

2 cups cold water
2 tablespoons arrowroot
2 to 3 tablespoons tamari

1
Heat a skillet and sauté the mushrooms in the oil for 2 minutes. Set the mushrooms aside.

2
Mix the water and arrowroot, and cook over medium heat until thick, whisking to avoid lumps. Add the mushrooms to the sauce, stir in the tamari, and cook until bubbling.

Per serving (with gravy): Calories 215, Total Protein 12 g, Soy Protein 10 g, Fat 9 g, Carbohydrates 19 g, Calcium 191 mg, Fiber 4 g, Sodium 841 mg

Chinese Sweet & Sour Balls

Yield: 6 servings (sixteen 1½-inch balls)

1

Preheat the oven to 350°F.

2

Whip together the peanut butter and tamari.

3

Mash the tofu in a bowl, and mix in the flour, peanut butter mixture, green pepper, mushrooms, water chestnuts, and green onions.

4

Form into sixteen 1½-inch balls, and arrange in an 8 x 8-inch pan spread with 1 tablespoon oil. Bake 20 minutes, then carefully turn each one over, and bake 20 minutes more. Serve on rice with Sweet and Sour Sauce, below.

1 tablespoon peanut butter
1 tablespoon tamari

1 pound firm tofu
½ cup whole wheat flour
½ cup finely chopped green peppers
¼ cup sliced fresh mushrooms
¼ cup sliced fresh water chestnuts or celery
4 green onions, thinly sliced

1

Combine all the ingredients in a saucepan, whisking out all lumps. Bring to a boil over medium-low heat, stirring constantly until thickened.

Sweet & Sour Sauce

1 cup unsweetened pineapple juice
6 tablespoons sweetener of your choice
6 tablespoons apple cider vinegar
2 tablespoons tamari
1½ tablespoons arrowroot or cornstarch
¼ teaspoon garlic powder

Per serving: Calories 214, Total Protein 8 g, Soy Protein 6 g, Fat 4 g, Carbohydrates 34 g, Calcium 97 mg, Fiber 2 g, Sodium 511 mg

Jerk Tofu or Tempeh

Jerk is a Jamaican way of spicing food that usually involves very hot peppers, among other spices. A prepared jerk sauce can be used, or try the one below, and adjust the heat to your own taste. Scotch bonnet peppers are the ones used in Jamaica, but they are extremely hot on the hot pepper scale. A little jalapeño works for hot pepper wimps.

Yield 4 to 6 servings

Tofu

Jerk Sauce:
¼ cup apple or papaya juice
3 tablespoons grated onion
3 cloves garlic, minced
2 tablespoons tamari
2 tablespoons minced fresh hot
    pepper of choice
2 tablespoons vinegar
1 tablespoon oil
1 tablespoon grated fresh
    gingerroot
1½ teaspoons allspice
½ teaspoon cinnamon
½ teaspoon freshly ground black
    pepper
½ teaspoon thyme
¼ teaspoon nutmeg

1 pound steamed tempeh or
    frozen firm tofu
½ cup green onions, chopped

1

If using frozen tofu, thaw and squeeze out the excess water.

2

Mix all the ingredients together in a blender, except the tempeh and green onions.

3

Cut the tempeh or tofu into 1-inch cubes or ½-inch strips, and arrange one layer deep in a glass pan. Pour the blended mixture over the top. Press the jerk sauce into the tofu with a spatula or the palm of your hands. Let it marinate for a few hours or overnight.

4

Preheat the oven to broil, prepare the coals in the grill, or heat the griddle. Broil for about 5 minutes, turn the pieces over, and broil 5 more minutes. If you are cooking on a grill or oiled griddle, brown on both sides. Serve hot with chopped green onions for garnish.

Per serving (with tempeh): Calories 222, Total Protein 18 g, Soy Protein 18 g, Fat 9 g, Carbohydrates 19 g, Calcium 98 mg, Fiber 5 g, Sodium 409 mg
Per serving (with tofu): Calories 110, Total Protein 7 g, Soy Protein 7 g, Fat 7 g, Carbohydrates 5 g, Calcium 109 mg, Fiber 1 g, Sodium 410 mg

Korean Barbeque Tofu

Yield: 6 servings

Tofu

1

Combine the marinade ingredients and marinate the sliced tofu at least 2 hours. (Marinating overnight is best.)

2

Brown the tofu on both sides in the oil. Garnish with chopped green onions, mushrooms, and/or snow peas, and serve with rice.

Marinade:
½ cup tamari
6 tablespoons sugar or sweetener of your choice
2 teaspoons dry mustard
4 cloves garlic, finely minced, or ½ teaspoon garlic powder
2 teaspoons onion powder

1½ pounds firm tofu, cut into ¼-inch slices

2 tablespoons oil

Options for Garnish:
Chopped green onions
Chopped mushrooms
Chopped snow peas

Per serving: Calories 156, Total Protein 9 g, Soy Protein 9 g, Fat 9 g, Carbohydrates 9 g, Calcium 122 mg, Fiber 0 g, Sodium 678 mg

Lasagne from the Garden

This delicious lasagne is bound to become a favorite for company dinners. Your guests will find it difficult to believe that it was made not only without meat, but without cheese!

Yield: 8 servings

Tofu

15 whole wheat, spinach, or regular lasagne noodles, cooked, rinsed, and drained

Lasagne Sauce:
1 large onion, minced
4 cloves garlic, minced
1 large carrot, scrubbed and minced
1 medium zucchini, grated, or ½ large eggplant, minced
½ pound mushrooms, sliced
1 (28-ounce) can diced tomatoes and their juice
1 (6-ounce) can tomato paste
½ cup dry red wine, or ½ cup water plus 1 tablespoon balsamic vinegar
2 teaspoons dried basil, or 2 tablespoons chopped fresh basil
1 teaspoon dried oregano, or 1 tablespoon chopped fresh oregano
1 teaspoon salt
1 teaspoon sweetener of your choice
Freshly ground black pepper, to taste

1

To make the sauce, mince the vegetables in a food processor or by hand. In a large, heavy pot, braise the onion, garlic, carrots, zucchini, and mushrooms in a little water until they are barely soft. Add the tomatoes, tomato paste, wine, herbs, salt, sweetener, and black pepper. Bring to a boil, reduce the heat, and let simmer, uncovered, while you make the filling and topping.

2

To make the filling, combine all the filling ingredients thoroughly, and set aside.

3

To make the Tangy Cream Sauce, bring the water, potato, onion, and salt to a boil in a small pot. Cover, lower the heat to a simmer, and cook until the potato is tender. Pour into a blender or food processor along with the crumbled tofu, nutritional yeast, lemon juice, and garlic powder, and blend until very smooth. Set aside. Preheat the oven to 350°F.

4

To assemble the lasagne, evenly spread ¼ of the tomato sauce on the bottom of a 9 x 13-inch baking pan. Top with 5 of the noodles, then ½ of the filling and a sprinkling of soy Parmesan, if you like. Spread on another ¼ of the tomato sauce, 5 more noodles, and the remaining filling (with a little more Parmesan). Top with another ¼ of the tomato sauce, then the remaining 5 noodles. Spread the remaining tomato sauce over the top, along with a little more Parmesan, if using. Top with the Tangy Cream Sauce. (You may not have room for all of it.) Finish by sprinkling on the fresh breadcrumbs.

5

Bake for 40 minutes; if it seems to be browning too quickly, cover with foil. Let the casserole stand for 10 minutes before serving.

Filling:
3 (12.3-ounce) packages extra-firm silken tofu, well mashed
1 (10-ounce) package frozen chopped spinach, thawed and squeezed dry, or 1 cup minced fresh parsley
½ cup soymilk
1 teaspoon salt
Pinch of ground nutmeg

Tangy Cream Sauce:
1½ cups water
1 medium potato, peeled and cut into chunks
½ medium onion, peeled and cut into chunks
1 teaspoon salt

¼ pound firm tofu, crumbled
¼ cup nutritional yeast flakes
1 tablespoon lemon juice
Pinch of garlic powder

Soy Parmesan (optional)
Breadcrumbs for topping

Per serving: Calories 379, Total Protein 24 g, Soy Protein 11 g, Fat 6 g, Carbohydrates 55 g, Calcium 190 mg, Fiber 13 g, Sodium 940 mg

Mattar Tofu

One of the best-loved Indian restaurant dishes is mattar panir, a tomato-flavored mixture of green peas and cubes of fresh cheese. Firm tofu makes an excellent substitute for the cheese. Serve this with rice for a complete meal.

Yield: 4 servings

Tofu

¾ pound firm tofu, cut into ½-inch cubes

2 tablespoons grated fresh gingerroot, or 1 teaspoon powdered ginger
1 tablespoon chopped fresh garlic
1 medium onion, minced

1 tablespoon garam masala or curry powder
1 teaspoon salt
1 teaspoon turmeric
1 teaspoon ground coriander
Pinch of cayenne
¼ cup water or vegetable stock

1 (14-ounce) can diced tomatoes with juice
1½ cups frozen baby peas (petit pois)
1 teaspoon liquid sweetener, sugar, or alternate

1

Dry-fry the tofu cubes in a large, non-stick skillet over high heat until they are golden on two sides. Remove from the pan and set aside.

2

Add the ginger and garlic to the hot pan, and steam-fry over high heat with a little bit of water for 1 minute. Add the onion and steam-fry until it is soft, about 5 minutes. Add the seasonings and ¼ cup water or stock, and stir well.

3

Add the tomatoes, peas, tofu, and sweetener, and simmer 10 minutes. Serve over basmati or other rice.

Per serving: Calories 198, Total Protein 14 g, Soy Protein 9 g, Fat 4 g, Carbohydrates 27 g, Calcium 47 mg, Fiber 7 g, Sodium 583 mg

Sesame Tofu

Yield: 4 to 6 servings

1

Preheat the oven to 350°F.

2

Grind the sesame seeds and flour together in a food processor or blender, and transfer to a bowl.

3

To make the sauce, chop the ginger-root and garlic in a food processor or blender, then add the tamari and water, and process until blended.

4

Dip each tofu slice into the sauce, then dredge in the flour-sesame mixture. Arrange the slices on a cookie sheet spread with the oil. Sprinkle any leftover sauce over the slices, then any leftover flour mixture. Bake 20 minutes on one side, then flip and bake 10 minutes on the other side. Serve hot with rice.

⅓ cup sesame seeds
⅓ cup unbleached white flour

Ginger Sauce:
1 inch cube gingerroot
2 cloves garlic
2 tablespoons tamari
2 tablespoons water

1 pound firm tofu, cut into ¼-inch slices
1 tablespoon oil

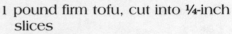

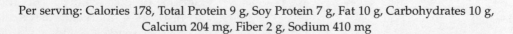

Per serving: Calories 178, Total Protein 9 g, Soy Protein 7 g, Fat 10 g, Carbohydrates 10 g, Calcium 204 mg, Fiber 2 g, Sodium 410 mg

Soy "Fish Cakes"

These "cakes" are very tasty, with a mild seafood flavor, and they are a good way to use up that last 2 cups of leftover cooked rice. The plain ones make great "fish burgers," served on buns. Some exotic flavor options are also included. Freeze any leftovers (the uncooked mixture or the cooked patties) for future meals.

Yield: 20 cakes

Tofu

1 pound medium-firm tofu, frozen, thawed, well squeezed, and finely crumbled
2 cups cooked short-grain brown rice
1 small onion, minced
6 tablespoons nutritional yeast flakes
2 tablespoons minced celery

Blended Mixture:
¼ pound medium-firm regular tofu
2½ tablespoons tamari
2 tablespoons water
1 tablespoon lemon juice
1 tablespoon herbal salt, or 2 tablespoons light miso
1 teaspoon kelp powder
½ teaspoon dry mustard
½ teaspoon dill weed
¼ teaspoon white pepper
Pinch celery seed

¼ cup unbleached white flour or vital wheat gluten

1
Mix the thawed tofu, rice, onion, nutritional yeast, and celery in a large bowl.

2
Combine the blended mixture ingredients in a blender or food processor until smooth. Add this to the bowl, along with the flour. Mix well with your hands. (You can make this ahead of time, and refrigerate it until you are ready to cook the patties.) Form 20 thin patties and cook on a nonstick skillet over medium-low heat for about 6 minutes per side, covering the skillet while cooking the first side.

3
As an alternative, you can place the patties on lightly greased or nonstick cookie sheets, and bake at 400°F for 7 minutes per side.

4
To make a crunchy outside coating on the patties, coat them with Seasoned Coating Mix (page 93), and bake using the oven method described above. Serve "fish cakes" alone, or on buns or toast, with Tartar Sauce (page 66), ketchup, or chile sauce. The mixture can also be shaped like "fish sticks," if you like, instead of patties.

Cajun-Style "Fish Cakes": Add ½ cup minced green onions, 2 teaspoons Cajun seasoning, and 2 crushed cloves of garlic.

Thai "Fish Cakes": Add 1 tablespoon Thai red chile paste, 4 cloves crushed garlic, and ½ cup chopped green beans or peas to the tofu-rice mixture. Top with a vinegar sauce made by mixing ½ cup vinegar, ⅓ cup minced onions, 2 tablespoons sugar, 2 tablespoons minced fresh basil or cilantro, 2 tablespoons grated carrot, and 1 small dried red chile, crushed.

Indian-Style "Fish Cakes": Add 2 tablespoons grated fresh gingerroot, 2 tablespoons minced cilantro, 1 tablespoon minced fresh mint, 2 cloves crushed garlic, and a pinch EACH of curry powder, cayenne, turmeric, coriander, and red chile pepper flakes to the tofu-rice mixture.

Jamaican-Style "Fish Cakes": Add 2 tablespoons chopped jalapeños and 2 teaspoons paprika to the tofu-rice mix.

1

To make the Seasoned Coating Mix, Thoroughly combine all the ingredients and store in a tightly covered container in the refrigerator.

Seasoned Coating Mix

1 cup soft whole wheat bread
   crumbs or finely crumbled,
   whole grain cold cereal
¼ cup cornmeal
2 teaspoons paprika
1 teaspoon salt (herbal or
   seasoned, if desired)
½ teaspoon black pepper
½ teaspoon ground sage
½ teaspoon dried thyme
½ teaspoon dried basil

Per cake: Calories 68, Total Protein 5 g, Soy Protein 3 g, Fat 1 g, Carbohydrates 9 g, Calcium 10 mg, Fiber 1 g, Sodium 131 mg

Stuffed Jumbo Shells

Tofu

Yield: 10 shells

4 ounces jumbo macaroni shells

1½ pounds firm regular tofu,
   mashed, or 1 pound tofu,
   mashed, and ½ pound soy
   mozzarella cheese, grated
¼ cup chopped fresh parsley
2 tablespoons onion powder
1½ teaspoons salt
½ teaspoon garlic powder
½ teaspoon basil

3 cups of your favorite tomato
sauce

Soy Parmesan cheese (optional)

1

Boil the macaroni shells in salted water to al dente.

2

Mix the rest of the ingredients except the tomato sauce.

3

Preheat the oven to 350°F. Spread 2 cups of the tomato sauce in a 9 x 9-inch pan. Spoon the tofu mixture into the cooked shells, about ⅓ cup per shell, and arrange in the pan. Add ½ cup water to the remaining sauce, then pour stripes of sauce over the top of the shells. Top with soy Parmesan cheese, if desired. Bake until the tomato sauce is bubbly, about 25 minutes.

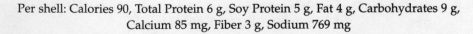

Per shell: Calories 90, Total Protein 6 g, Soy Protein 5 g, Fat 4 g, Carbohydrates 9 g,
Calcium 85 mg, Fiber 3 g, Sodium 769 mg

Szechuan Bean Curd

If you like hot foods, you'll love this simple, super-fast Chinese dish. Serve with rice or noodles and steamed or stir-fried vegetables, or as part of a larger Chinese meal.

Szechuan peppercorns have a distinctive flavor. Look for them in health food stores, Asian grocery stores, or the Chinese food section of large supermarkets. Toast them in a hot, dry skillet until they are aromatic, then grind in a blender or spice grinder, and store in an airtight container.

Yield: 6 servings

Tofu

1

Steam-fry the mushrooms and onions in a hot, lightly oiled or nonstick medium skillet or wok for a couple of minutes.

2

Add the tofu cubes and a mixture of the sherry, chile paste, tamari, and black bean sauce. Stir over high heat for 3 to 4 minutes.

3

Add the dissolved cornstarch and stir to thicken. Sprinkle with the Szechuan pepper, if you have it, and serve with rice or hot wheat tortillas.

Note: If you have time, you can use 6 dried Chinese mushrooms, reconstituted in hot water, instead of fresh mushrooms. After soaking, remove the stems and discard them. Use 2 tablespoons of the soaking water to dissolve the cornstarch.

6 large, brown cultivated or shiitake mushrooms, chopped
6 green onions, cut into short lengths
1½ pounds medium-firm tofu, cut into ½-inch cubes
¼ cup dry sherry (or non-alcoholic alternative)
2 tablespoons Szechuan hot bean paste (Chinese chile bean paste)
2 tablespoons tamari
2 teaspoons Chinese black bean sauce
2 teaspoons cornstarch dissolved in 2 tablespoons cold water
Roasted ground Szechuan pepper, to taste (optional)

Per serving: Calories 171, Total Protein 15 g, Soy Protein 13 g, Fat 5 g, Carbohydrates 14 g, Calcium 11 mg, Fiber 3 g, Sodium 342 mg

Tofu Pizza

Tofu

1 (10-inch) ready-made pizza crust
1 cup your favorite tomato sauce
½ pound firm regular tofu, crumbled
1 cup sliced mushrooms
½ cup sliced olives
½ cup grated mozzarella cheese

1

Preheat the oven to 450°F.

2

Spread the pizza crust with the tomato sauce. Sprinkle on the tofu, mushrooms, olives, and cheese. Bake for 15 minutes or until the cheese is melted.

Per slice: Calories 157, Total Protein 8 g, Soy Protein 3 g, Fat 5 g, Carbohydrates 20 g, Calcium 142 mg, Fiber 1 g, Sodium 256 mg

Tofurkey

Tofu

1

Combine the ingredients for the sauce, and mix well.

2

Carefully place the tofu slices in a deep pan, and cover with the sauce. Set aside for at least 30 minutes to marinate.

3

Preheat the oven to 350°F. Pile the stuffing on a lightly oiled baking pan. Make a neat little pile of stuffing. Surround the stuffing with the tofu slices, layering them carefully one on top of the other. Don't worry about broken slices. Completely surround the stuffing, and continue layering the slices of tofu until they are all used up.

4

Firmly, but gently, with two hands, press the tofu down around the stuffing and apply pressure to help the slices and stuffing hold together. Mold into a turkey shape if desired. Decorate with carrot drumsticks. Bake uncovered for 1 hour.

Tofurkey Sauce:
¾ cup water
½ cup tamari
¼ cup olive oil
3 cloves crushed garlic
1 teaspoon ground sage
1 teaspoon ground thyme
½ teaspoon dry mustard
½ teaspoon oregano
½ teaspoon rosemary
Dash cayenne pepper

2 pounds firm regular tofu, drained and cut into thin slices

Your favorite stuffing

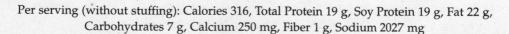

Per serving (without stuffing): Calories 316, Total Protein 19 g, Soy Protein 19 g, Fat 22 g, Carbohydrates 7 g, Calcium 250 mg, Fiber 1 g, Sodium 2027 mg

Tofu Spinach Pie

Yield: one 8-inch pie (8 servings)

Tofu

1 cup diced fresh mushrooms
2 medium onions, diced
¼ cup safflower oil
2 tablespoons chopped fresh
    parsley
2 tablespoons dill weed

1 (10-ounce) package fresh
    spinach, washed and chopped
Tamari to taste

2 cups firm regular tofu, drained
    and mashed

1 (8-inch) pie crust of your choice

Grated soy cheese of your
    choice, for topping (optional)

1

Sauté the mushrooms and onions in the oil for a few minutes. Add the parsley and dill weed and cook a few more minutes.

2

Add the spinach and tamari, stir, and cook a few more minutes.

3

Remove from the heat and add the tofu. Mix well and adjust the seasonings.

4

Prebake the pie crust at 400°F for 10 to 12 minutes until golden brown.

5

Fill the pie crust with the cooled tofu filling, top with grated soy cheese, if desired, and bake at 350°F for about 30 minutes.

Per serving: Calories 243, Total Protein 7 g, Soy Protein 4 g, Fat 16 g, Carbohydrates 17 g, Calcium 153 mg, Fiber 3 g, Sodium 103 mg

Tofu Tacos

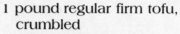
Yield: 2 cups filling (4 tacos)

1

Combine the tofu and taco seasoning, and brown in the oil. Serve in taco shells with the taco fixings.

Tostadas: Fry either corn or flour tortillas one at a time, in hot oil until crisp and golden. Drain on paper toweling. To build the tostada, start with the crisp tortillas, then the seasoned tofu, tomatoes, green peppers, and lettuce. Top with the grated soy cheese and chopped olives. Spoon on hot sauce to taste.

1 pound regular firm tofu, crumbled
1 (1¾ ounce) package taco seasoning mix
2 tablespoons oil

Taco Fixings:
Chopped tomatoes
Lettuce
Onion
Grated soy cheese (optional)
Chopped olives
Hot sauce

Per taco: Calories 146, Total Protein 8 g, Soy Protein 8 g, Fat 11 g, Carbohydrates 2 g, Calcium 119 mg, Fiber 0 g, Sodium 8 mg

Baked Enchiladas
with Beans & Tempeh

This takes time to make but the results are incredibly good.

Yield: 8 servings

Tempeh

12 large whole wheat tortillas

Enchilada Sauce:
3 tablespoons oil
2 onions, chopped
2 tablespoons chili powder
¾ teaspoon salt
1 teaspoon cumin
⅓ cup flour
5 cups water

½ pound tempeh, steamed for 15
  minutes
2 (15-ounce) cans pinto beans,
  undrained

1

To make the enchilada sauce, sauté the onions in the oil until they are soft. Sprinkle with the chili powder, salt, cumin, and flour, and cook for a few more minutes. Add the water, bring to a boil, then simmer over low heat for 20 minutes, stirring occasionally.

2

Grate the steamed tempeh and add to the sauce. Drain the beans and add the liquid to the sauce. Pour 1 cup of the sauce into the bottom of a lightly oiled 9 x 13-inch baking pan.

3

On a hot, dry griddle, cook each tortilla for 1 or 2 minutes on each side. Place a spoonful of the beans on each tortilla, and roll up. Place seam side down in the sauce. When all the tortillas are filled, pour the remaining sauce over the contents of the dish. Bake at 350°F for 30 minutes. If desired, top the casserole with 1 cup grated Jack cheese.

Per serving: Calories 398, Total Protein 16 g, Soy Protein 5 g, Fat 10 g, Carbohydrates 60 g, Calcium 97 mg, Fiber 8 g, Sodium 369 mg

Burritos with Tempeh Filling

Yield: 10 burritos

Tempeh

1

Grate the steamed tempeh and mix with the chili, garlic, and cumin.

2

Heat the oil in a skillet, and sauté the onion until it is soft. Stir in the tempeh mixture, and cook 10 more minutes.

3

Drain the beans and mash or process until smooth, adding a little bean liquid if they are too stiff. Stir the beans into the tempeh-onion mixture. Add salt or dash of cayenne, to taste. Keep the filling warm.

4

Heat a griddle or large skillet, and fry the tortillas 1 to 2 minutes on each side, pressing down with a spatula if they puff up. Keep the tortillas warm with a towel. When they are all cooked, place about ⅓ cup of the filling down the center of each tortilla. Sprinkle with chopped lettuce, chopped onion, and a spoonful of salsa. Fold the bottom third of the tortilla over the filling, then fold in one side toward the center. Fold the other side in to overlap.

½ pound tempeh, steamed for 20 minutes and cooled
1 tablespoon chili powder
½ teaspoon garlic powder
½ teaspoon cumin

2 tablespoons oil
1 onion, chopped

2 cups cooked pinto beans
Dash of salt or cayenne, to taste
10 (10-inch) whole wheat tortillas

Chopped lettuce
Chopped onion
Salsa

Make Ahead Burritos to Freeze: Use the same 10 whole wheat tortillas and filling. Make the filling but do not heat the tortillas. Place ⅓ cup filling down the center of each tortilla. Fold the sides in, then fold up the bottom and top like an envelope, moistening the edges to seal. Wrap individually in plastic and freeze. The burritos can be defrosted and heated through in a microwave, or thawed and baked in a conventional oven.

Per burrito: Calories 251, Total Protein 10 g, Soy Protein 4 g, Fat 8 g, Carbohydrates 34 g, Calcium 41 mg, Fiber 4 g, Sodium 206 mg

Chimichangas

Crisp and golden, these Mexican favorites melt in your mouth

Yield: 10 chimichangas

Tempeh

Filling:
1 large onion, chopped
2 cloves garlic, chopped
2 tablespoons oil
½ pound tempeh, steamed for 20
   minutes, cooled, and grated
1 teaspoon cumin
1 teaspoon oregano
½ teaspoon salt
1 (4-ounce) can green chilies,
   chopped

10 (10-inch) whole wheat tortillas

Oil for deep frying

1

In a skillet over medium-high heat, sauté the onion and in garlic the 2 tablespoons oil for 2 minutes. Add the tempeh, cumin, oregano, and salt. Remove from the heat and stir in the green chilies.

2

The tortillas must be soft and pliable. If not, sprinkle them with a few drops of water, and cook in a dry pan until softened, or wrap in plastic and heat in a microwave.

3

Place about ⅓ cup of the filling along one edge of a tortilla. Roll up, tucking in the sides to seal in the filling. Fasten with a wooden toothpick.

4

When all the tortillas are made, heat at least 2 inches of oil in a wok or deep, heavy skillet to 360°F. Fry 2 or 3 rolls at a time for 1 to 2 minutes on each side until golden. Lift out with a slotted spoon onto paper towels. (Do not use tongs.) Remove the toothpicks. Serve with salsa, guacamole, and shredded lettuce on the side.

Per chimichanga: Calories 209, Total Protein 8 g, Soy Protein 4 g, Fat 8 g,
Carbohydrates 26 g, Calcium 26 mg, Fiber 3 g, Sodium 313 mg

Hawaiian Kebabs

Exotic looking and wonderful to eat, these can be grilled outdoors or made in an oven.

Yield: 18 kebabs

1

Cut the fresh pineapple into 1-inch chunks, or drain the canned pineapple, saving the juice.

2

In a saucepan, combine the stock, tamari, lemon juice, oil, honey (if using), gingerroot, and arrowroot. Simmer the sauce a few minutes until thick and shiny.

3

Cut the steamed tempeh into thin 1-inch squares. Add to the sauce mixture, cover, and simmer for 5 minutes. Cool.

4

If desired, steam the onion and pepper for 1 minute to soften, then cool. Thread the skewers, alternating squares of tempeh, peppers, onions, and pineapple. If red peppers are not available, use cherry tomatoes for color. Brush the kebabs lightly with the oil.

5

Place the kebabs on a grill, and cook about 5 minutes on each side, or place in a broiling pan, and cook about 5 inches from the source of the heat, turning once and brushing with any leftover marinade.

1 pineapple or 1 (14-ounce) can pineapple chunks, in juice

Hawaiian Sauce:
½ cup vegetable stock or pineapple juice
2 tablespoons tamari
2 tablespoons lemon juice
1 teaspoon dark sesame oil
1 teaspoon honey (omit if using pineapple juice)
1 inch gingerroot, chopped
1 tablespoon arrowroot

½ pound tempeh, steamed for 15 minutes and cooled

1 onion, cut in large chunks
1 large green pepper, cut in 1-inch squares
1 sweet red pepper, cut in 1-inch squares

Skewers*
1 tablespoon oil

*If using bamboo skewers, soak them for 30 minutes in cold water to prevent burning.

Per kebab: Calories 57, Total Protein 3 g, Soy Protein 2 g, Fat 2 g, Carbohydrates 7 g, Calcium 19 mg, Fiber 1 g, Sodium 113 mg

Sweet & Sour Tempeh

Yield: 6 servings

Tempeh

½ pound tempeh, cut into thin
   1-inch squares
1 cup vegetable stock
1 tablespoon tamari
2 tablespoons oil

1 (15-ounce) can pineapple
   tidbits, in juice

1 green pepper, cut in 1-inch
   squares
1 onion, cut in thin half-moons
1 cup boiling water

¼ cup cider vinegar
2 tablespoons honey
2 tablespoons tamari
2 tablespoons arrowroot

1
Steam the tempeh for 10 minutes in the vegetable stock and tamari. Drain the tempeh, reserving the liquid for making the sauce. Heat the oil in a skillet, and sauté the tempeh until lightly browned.

2
Drain the pineapple and add the pineapple juice to the drained tempeh liquid.

3
Add the pepper and onion to the boiling water. Bring the water to a boil again, and drain.

4
To make the sauce, place the pineapple juice-tempeh liquid in a measuring cup, and add enough water to make 2 cups. Stir in the vinegar, honey, tamari, and arrowroot. Cook the sauce until thickened and bubbly, then combine with the pepper, onion, pineapple, and tempeh. Serve over hot rice.

Per serving: Calories 169, Total Protein 8 g, Soy Protein 7 g, Fat 3 g, Carbohydrates 28 g, Calcium 55 mg, Fiber 3 g, Sodium 507 mg

Tempeh or Taco-Style Fajitas

Yield: 6 fajitas

Tempeh

1

To make the tempeh filling, steam the tempeh for 10 minutes. Cool slightly and cut into long, thin strips. Combine the tamari and pressed garlic, pour over the tempeh strips, and marinate for 30 minutes. Heat a skillet and fry the marinated tempeh over medium high heat in the 2 tablespoons olive oil until brown. Remove to paper towels.

2

To make the taco-style filling, mix the wine vinegar, tamari, and garlic powder. Add the boiling water and pour the mixture over the textured soy protein. Cover and let stand for about 15 minutes. Sauté the textured soy protein in a hot skillet in the 2 tablespoons olive oil. Sprinkle with the remaining soaking liquid while cooking.

3

Warm each tortilla in a hot skillet for only a few seconds until soft.

4

Heat the 1 tablespoon oil in skillet, and cook the pepper strips a few minutes over medium high heat, then add the onions and cook until soft. Arrange on each tortilla a few strips of tempeh or a spoonful of the taco-style filling, pepper, and onion. Fold the bottom of the tortilla up, then fold two sides in.

Tempeh Filling:
½ pound tempeh
¼ cup tamari
2 garlic cloves, pressed
2 tablespoons olive oil

Taco-Style Filling:
1 tablespoon wine vinegar
1 tablespoon tamari
½ teaspoon garlic powder,
    or 1 clove garlic, minced
¾ cup boiling water
1 cup chunk style textured soy
    protein
2 tablespoons olive oil

6 whole wheat tortillas

1 tablespoon oil
1 green pepper, cut in long ½-inch
    strips
1 red pepper, cut in long ½-inch
    strips
1 onion, cut in rings

Per fajita (with tempeh filling): Calories 237, Total Protein 10 g, Soy Protein 7 g, Fat 11 g, Carbohydrates 24 g, Calcium 46 mg, Fiber 3 g, Sodium 784 mg
Per fajita (with taco-style filling): Calories 200, Total Protein 9 g, Soy Protein 7 g, Fat 8 g, Carbohydrates 21 g, Calcium 42 mg, Fiber 2 g, Sodium 282 mg

"Beef"-Style Taco or Burrito Filling

This also makes a tasty filling for Enchiladas (page 100).

Yield: 3 cups

Textured Soy

1 cup boiling water
2 tablespoons tamari
1 tablespoon chili powder
½ teaspoon oregano
1 cup textured soy protein
   granules

½ cup minced onion
½ cup minced green pepper
1 clove garlic, minced
Minced jalapeño to taste (optional)
1 tablespoon olive oil

1

Mix the boiling water, tamari, chili powder, and oregano, and pour over the textured soy protein granules. Cover and let stand for about 10 minutes.

2

Briefly sauté the onion, green pepper, garlic, and jalapeño in the olive oil. Add the textured soy protein mixture, and continue to cook until browned. Serve hot in tacos or burritos with all the fixings.

Variation: Add 1½ cups cooked pinto beans, or 1 (16-ounce) can, drained, to the mixture, and simmer until heated.

Per ½ cup: Calories: 74, Total Protein: 7 g., Soy Protein: 7 g., Fat: 2 g., Carbohydrates: 6 g.,
Calcium: 39 mg., Fiber 2 g., Sodium: 339 mg.

Herbed Loaf

Leftover loaf can be sliced for sandwiches or a cold cut platter.

Yield: 8 servings

1

Pour the boiling water over the textured soy granules in a bowl, and mix in the ketchup and basil. Let stand for 10 minutes.

2

Sauté the onions in the oil in a small frying pan until soft. Combine with the soy granules mixture and the remaining ingredients.

3

Preheat the oven to 350°F. Lightly oil a loaf or bread pan, and pack the mixture in tightly, smoothing the top. Bake for 45 minutes. If the loaf begins to get too brown on top, cover with foil. After removing from the oven, let the loaf set in the pan for 10 minutes, then run a knife around the edges to loosen, and turn out onto a platter. Garnish with lemon slices and sprigs of parsley, and top with tomato sauce or mushroom gravy.

2½ cups boiling water
3 cups textured soy protein granules
¼ cup ketchup
1 teaspoon basil

½ cup finely chopped onions
2 tablespoons olive oil
¾ cup unbleached white or whole wheat flour
½ cup finely minced parsley
1 teaspoon salt
½ teaspoon garlic powder
½ teaspoon oregano
½ teaspoon marjoram
¼ teaspoon pepper

Per serving: Calories: 178, Total Protein: 16 g., Soy Protein: 15 g., Fat: 4 g., Carbohydrates: 20 g., Calcium: 104 mg., Fiber 3 g., Sodium: 354 mg.

Moussaka

This is a vegan version of a three-layered dish that is a Mediterranean classic. Traditionally it is served lukewarm or at room temperature, so it can be made ahead to delight your guests.

Yield: 6 to 8 servings

1 large eggplant, peeled and sliced (about 1 pound)
⅓ cup unbleached white flour
1 teaspoon paprika
½ teaspoon salt
⅛ teaspoon cayenne

Tomato Sauce:
⅞ cup boiling water
1 cup soy protein granules or flakes
1 tablespoon olive oil
1 large onion, chopped
1 (16-ounce) can stewed tomatoes
2 tablespoons minced parsley
1 teaspoon oregano
1 teaspoon basil
½ teaspoon cinnamon
½ teaspoon nutmeg
½ teaspoon salt

1

Place the eggplant slices in a large bowl, sprinkling them with salt as you layer them. Place a plate over the slices, and weight it down with a heavy pan. Let the slices set for 30 minutes, then rinse and pat dry on a towel.

2

Combine the flour, paprika, ½ teaspoon salt, and cayenne in a shallow bowl, and dredge the eggplant slices in the mixture. Heat a nonstick skillet and and use a pastry brush or paper towel to coat the pan with a little olive oil. Fry the eggplant slices until lightly browned. It's alright if some of the flour still shows. Arrange the fried slices in a 9 x 9-inch pan.

3

To make the sauce, pour the boiling water over the soy granules or flakes in a small bowl, and set aside to soak. In a medium saucepan, sauté the onion in the 1 tablespoon olive oil until soft. Purée the stewed tomatoes, parsley, oregano, basil, cinnamon, nutmeg, and salt briefly in a blender, and add to the onion. Stir in the reconstituted soy granules, and simmer the sauce for a few minutes to blend the flavors.

4

To make the Creamy Topping, combine the tofu, ¼ cup olive oil, nutritional yeast, ½ teaspoon salt, and lemon juice in a food processor or blender until smooth and creamy. Preheat the oven to 375°F.

5

To assemble the moussaka, pour the tomato sauce over the eggplant slices and cover with the bread crumbs. Spread the blended tofu mixture evenly on top, smoothing with a spatula. Bake the moussaka for about 50 minutes. The top will be a light golden brown. Let the moussaka stand for at least 10 minutes after you remove it from the oven.

Creamy Topping:
1 pound firm silken tofu
¼ cup olive oil
¼ cup nutritional yeast flakes
½ teaspoon salt
Juice of 1 lemon (2 tablespoons)

1 cup soft bread crumbs

Per serving: Calories 250, Total Protein 15 g, Soy Protein 10 g, Fat 12 g, Carbohydrates 22 g, Calcium 119 mg, Fiber 5 g, Sodium 525 mg

Mushroom Stroganoff

Enjoy these delicious chunks in a flavorful, creamy sauce with mushrooms and onions.

Yield: 6 servings

Textured
Soy

1½ cups boiling water
1 cup textured soy protein
   chunks
2 tablespoons ketchup

1 cup thinly sliced onions
2 tablespoons margarine
1 cup sliced mushrooms

Sauce:
1 tablespoon margarine
1 tablespoon unbleached white
   flour
1 cup vegetable stock
1 tablespoon ketchup
2 tablespoons Mock Sour Cream
   (page 34)
Salt, to taste

1

Pour the boiling water over the textured soy chunks in a saucepan, and mix in the 2 tablespoons ketchup. Let stand for 10 minutes, then cover and simmer for 20 minutes.

2

Meanwhile, slowly sauté the onions in the 2 tablespoons margarine over low heat for 15 minutes, then add the mushrooms, and cook a few minutes more.

3

To make the sauce, melt the 1 tablespoon margarine in a small saucepan, and stir in the flour. Cook a minute or two, then gradually stir in the vegetable stock, and cook until bubbly. Remove from the heat, and stir in the 1 tablespoon ketchup and the sour cream. Add salt to taste.

4

Add the cooked, drained soy chunks and the mushrooms and onions to the sauce. Serve over noodles or rice.

Per serving: Calories 127, Total Protein 8 g, Soy Protein 7 g, Fat 6 g, Carbohydrates 10 g, Calcium 46 mg, Fiber 2 g, Sodium 203 mg

Potato Hash with Soy Protein

This is a hearty, stick-to-the-ribs kind of breakfast, brunch, lunch, or supper dish.

Yield: 3 cups (3 to 4 servings)

Textured
Soy

1

Mix the boiling water and tamari, pour over the textured soy protein, and let stand for 10 minutes.

2

Mix the textured soy with all the remaining ingredients, except the olive oil. Fry the hash in the olive oil in a nonstick pan until the potatoes are tender and browned, turning as needed. Serve hot with ketchup.

6 tablespoons boiling water
1 tablespoon tamari
½ cup textured soy protein
   granules

4 cups grated potatoes
¼ cup chopped onions
¼ cup chopped green pepper
1 clove garlic, minced
2 tablespoons minced parsley or
   chives
¼ teaspoon freshly ground black
   pepper

1 tablespoon olive oil

Per serving: Calories 194, Total Protein 8 g, Soy Protein 6 g, Fat 4 g, Carbohydrates 31 g, Calcium 47 mg, Fiber 4 g, Sodium 298 mg

Shepherd's Pie

Textured Soy

Yield: 6 servings

Use either:
4 cups boiling water
2 cups textured soy protein
chunks
2 tablespoons ketchup

or

2 pounds frozen firm tofu,
defrosted, squeezed dry, and
cut into ½-inch cubes
½ cup tamari

4 potatoes, cut into ½-inch cubes

2 tablespoons olive oil
1 medium onion, chopped
½ cup chopped celery
¼ cup unbleached white flour
2 cups vegetable stock
½ teaspoon salt
½ teaspoon oregano or thyme
½ teaspoon marjoram
½ teaspoon garlic powder

1½ cups cooked sliced carrots
1 cup cooked or frozen peas

1

If using the soy chunks, pour the boiling water over the chunks in a saucepan, and mix in the ketchup. Cover and simmer for about 20 minutes or until tender.

2

If using the frozen tofu, pour the tamari over the cubes in a bowl, and stir well to coat. Set aside.

3

Cook the cubed potatoes in enough water to cover until tender.

4

Meanwhile, sauté the onion in the 2 tablespoons olive oil for several minutes, then add the celery and sauté a few minutes more. Sprinkle the flour over the onions and celery, stir in, and cook for 2 minutes, then slowly stir in the vegetable stock to make a sauce. When it comes to a boil, add the ½ teaspoon salt, oregano or thyme, marjoram, and garlic powder.

5

Combine the sauce with the soy chunks or tofu cubes, the cooked carrots, and peas. Pour into a 3-quart casserole. Preheat the oven to 350°F.

6

Drain the potatoes, mash, and add the olive oil or margarine, ½ teaspoon salt, and enough soymilk to make the potatoes smooth and spreadable. Spread the potatoes over the top of the chunks and vegetables, and sprinkle with paprika. Place the pie on a cookie sheet to catch any drippings, and bake for about 30 minutes until the potatoes have browned and the filling is bubbling. You can make the pie ahead and refrigerate it until ready to cook; just bake the pie a little longer.

1 tablespoon olive oil or margarine
½ teaspoon salt
Soymilk for mashing the potatoes
Paprika for topping

Per serving (with textured soy): Calories 233, Total Protein 16 g, Soy Protein 13 g, Fat 7 g, Carbohydrates 25 g, Calcium 108 mg, Fiber 6 g, Sodium 557 mg
Per serving (with tofu): Calories 275, Total Protein 16 g, Soy Protein 13 g, Fat 13 g, Carbohydrates 22 g, Calcium 206 mg, Fiber 4 g, Sodium 1901 mg

Stuffed Cabbage Rolls

Soy granules make a healthful version of this robust ethnic favorite.

Yield: 12 rolls

Textured Soy

4 large shiitake mushrooms, stems removed and chopped

⅞ cup boiling water
1 cup textured soy protein granules
1 tablespoon ketchup

1 large head cabbage

1 cup chopped onions
1 clove garlic, minced
1 tablespoon olive oil
1 cup cooked brown rice
1 teaspoon salt
¼ teaspoon mace or nutmeg
½ teaspoon coriander

1 (16-ounce) can chopped tomatoes, undrained
1 teaspoon honey

1

Chop the shiitake mushrooms and set aside.

2

Pour the boiling water over the soy granules, mix in the ketchup, and set aside to soak.

3

Remove the center core from the cabbage. Place the cabbage head in a colander, and pour hot water over it to loosen the leaves. Cool slightly. Remove 12 leaves and cut out the hard center rib from each leaf.

4

Sauté the onion and garlic in the olive oil until soft. To make the filling, combine the onions and garlic with the chopped shiitake, soaked granules, cooked brown rice, salt, mace or nutmeg, and coriander.

5

Make a sauce by combining the canned tomatoes and their juice, and the honey in a blender.

6

Preheat the oven to 350°F. Place a cabbage leaf on a work surface with the inside of the leaf facing up. Fill with about 2 tablespoons of the filling mixture, fold the sides of the leaf into the center, and roll up. Place seam side down in a lightly oiled 11 x 9-inch casserole dish or baking pan. Spoon the sauce over the rolls, cover the pan with foil, and bake for 35 to 40 minutes.

Per roll: Calories: 98, Total Protein: 5 g., Soy Protein: 3 g., Fat: 1 g., Carbohydrates: 16 g., Calcium: 64 mg., Fiber 3 g., Sodium: 209 mg.

Zesty Italian Spaghetti Balls

This mixture can also be shaped into patties or burgers and served in buns.

Yield: 20 balls

1

Pour the boiling water over the soy granules, and let stand for 10 minutes.

2

In a skillet, sauté the onion in the olive oil for a few minutes until soft. Add the soaked soy granules and stir in the chili powder, garlic powder, oregano, salt, and tamari. Mix in the flour and combine well.

3

Shape into 1½-inch balls, pressing firmly with your hands. When the balls are formed, brown them lightly in a little bit of oil in a hot skillet, rolling them over carefully to keep them round and brown them evenly.

4

To reduce the fat content of the balls, bake them on a nonstick cookie sheet at 350°F until lightly browned instead of frying them.

1¾ cups boiling water
2 cups textured soy protein
   granules

½ cup finely chopped onions
2 tablespoons olive oil
½ teaspoon chili powder
½ teaspoon garlic powder
½ teaspoon oregano
1 teaspoon salt
1 tablespoon tamari
½ cup unbleached white flour

Oil for frying

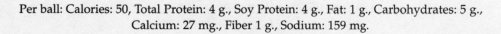

Per ball: Calories: 50, Total Protein: 4 g., Soy Protein: 4 g., Fat: 1 g., Carbohydrates: 5 g., Calcium: 27 mg., Fiber 1 g., Sodium: 159 mg.

Baked Soybeans

This is a delicious way to serve leftover beans.

Yield: 4 cups (6 servings)

Soybeans

1 medium onion, chopped
1 small green pepper, chopped
2 cloves garlic, minced
½ tablespoon soy or olive oil
3 cups Pressure Cooked
   Soybeans (page 28)
¼ cup sorghum molasses
¼ cup ketchup or tomato paste
1 teaspoon salt
½ teaspoon dry mustard

1

Preheat the oven to 350°F.

2

Sauté the onion, green pepper, and garlic in the oil. Mix with all the remaining ingredients in a 1½-quart casserole dish, and bake uncovered for about 45 minutes. (If you don't have time for baking, heat thoroughly on the stovetop or in the microwave.)

Variation: Add 2 soy "hot dogs" cut in chunks to the casserole mixture before baking.

Per serving: Calories 229, Total Protein 13 g, Soy Protein 12 g, Fat 8 g, Carbohydrates 26 g, Calcium 116 mg, Fiber 4 g, Sodium 480 mg

Barbecue Soybeans

Add your favorite barbecue sauce to cooked soybeans, heat, and serve.

Yield: 4 cups (6 servings)

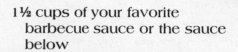

Soybeans

1

Combine all the ingredients, except the beans and vinegar. Heat and bring to a boil. Reduce the heat and simmer for 10 minutes.

2

Stir in the beans and vinegar, and simmer until heated through.

1½ cups of your favorite barbecue sauce or the sauce below

Barbecue Sauce:
1 (4-ounce) can tomato paste
1 cup water
⅓ cup brown sugar
¼ cup salad mustard
1 tablespoon onion powder
½ teaspoon garlic powder
½ teaspoon allspice
½ teaspoon cracked red pepper, or chipotle, to taste
½ teaspoon salt

3 cups cooked soybeans

2 tablespoons vinegar

Per serving: Calories 212, Total Protein 13 g, Soy Protein 12 g, Fat 9 g, Carbohydrates 19 g, Calcium 103 mg, Fiber 4 g, Sodium 474 mg

Soybean Burritos

Use wheat or corn tortillas, and add chopped tomatoes and jalapeños or your favorite salsa. Sprinkle on nutritional yeast for a cheese-like flavor.

Yield: 8 burritos

Soybeans

Wheat or corn tortillas
Pressure Cooked Soybeans
  (page 28)
Your favorite salsa
Chopped tomatoes
Chopped hot peppers, to taste
Chopped lettuce
Chopped fresh cilantro
Nutritional yeast flakes

1

Heat the tortillas on a hot griddle for a few moments. Fill the tortillas with the beans and fixings of choice.

Per burrito (using ⅓ cup for all ingredients): Calories 223, Total Protein 13 g, Soy Protein 8 g, Fat 5 g, Carbohydrates 31 g, Calcium 102 mg, Fiber 6 g, Sodium 216 mg

Soybean-Roasted Pepper Pasta

Yield: 6 servings

Soybeans

1
Cook the soybeans in salted water for 5 minutes, then drain. Rinse with cold water and set aside.

2
Roast the pepper in a 400°F oven until golden brown (about 30 minutes). Turn it once during roasting. Remove from the oven, place it in a brown paper bag, and let sweat for 5 minutes. Peel, cut into strips, and set aside.

3
Cook the fettuccini according to the package directions in a large pot of water.

4
Sauté the tofu cubes and garlic in the olive oil until lightly browned. Add the green soybeans, pepper strips, greens, and wine. Cover and cook a few minutes until the greens begin to wilt (about 4 minutes). Season with salt and pepper.

5
Mix the cooked pasta and cooked vegetables. Toss with the fresh basil, and serve with fresh lemon wedges on the side.

1½ cups green vegetable soybeans
1 red bell pepper
1 pound fettuccini
¼ pound firm tofu, cut in ½-inch cubes
6 cloves garlic, thinly sliced
3 tablespoons olive oil
1 bunch salad savoy or your favorite greens, cleaned and trimmed
⅓ cup white wine or vegetable stock

Salt and pepper, to taste
¼ cup chopped fresh basil
Lemon wedges for garnish

Per serving: Calories 265, Total Protein 12 g, Soy Protein 7 g, Fat 9 g, Carbohydrates 32 g, Calcium 117 mg, Fiber 3 g, Sodium 11 mg

Crêpes with Shiitake Filling

Yield: 10 Crêpes

Filling:
2 teaspoons olive oil
½ cup chopped sweet pepper
1 medium onion, chopped
5 cups chopped fresh shiitake
    mushrooms
2 tablespoons tamari

Crêpes:
1⅔ cups unbleached white flour
⅔ cup nutritional yeast flakes
½ cup soy protein isolate
½ teaspoon salt
2¾ cup water
½ cup soymilk

Oil for cooking crêpes

1

In a large skillet, sauté the filling ingredients for 10 to 15 minutes until all the liquid is absorbed. Keep covered to keep warm.

2

In a medium mixing bowl, whisk together all the crêpe ingredients, except the oil for cooking, until a smooth batter is formed. Heat a cast-iron skillet over medium heat, and squirt a scant ¼ teaspoon of the oil on the pan just before you're ready to cook your crêpe. With a soup ladle, pour ⅓ cup of batter around on the pan, and tilt the pan so an even, 8-inch round crepe is formed. Cook until light brown on each side, and remove to a plate. Cover the crêpes with a towel to keep them soft. Repeat the procedure until all the crêpes are made. It takes less time if you use 2 pans to cook the crêpes.

3

Spoon about ½ cup of the filling down the middle of each crêpe, and roll them up tight. Place them on a serving platter, and serve hot. These are good served with fresh salsa.

Per crêpe: Calories 180, Total Protein 13 g, Soy Protein 5 g, Fat 2 g, Carbohydrates 29 g, Calcium 99 mg, Fiber 1 g, Sodium 366 mg

Side Dishes

Green Soybeans in the Pod

These are a special snack treat in parts of Asia, served as an appetizer, an accompaniment to sake or beer, or a lunch box treat for children. The beans are harvested in the pod when they are almost mature but are still green and have not dried out. If you have garden space, they are easy to grow during the warm season. Green soybeans can sometimes be found in Asian or natural foods stores.

Yield: about 2 cups

Soybeans

Wash the soybeans, then steam or boil them in their pods in the water and salt for about 15 to 20 minutes or until crisp-tender. Serve in the pod but remove from the pod before eating.

Variation: Remove the soybeans from the pods, and steam or boil for about 15 to 20 minutes until crisp-tender. Serve as you would green peas.

1 pound green soybeans in the pod
2 cups water
½ teaspoon salt

Per ¼ cup: Calories 80, Total Protein 7 g, Soy Protein 7 g, Fat 2 g, Carbohydrates 6 g, Calcium 84 mg, Fiber 1 g, Sodium 135 mg

Potato Fritters

These are easy to make and so yummy. They are delicious served with applesauce or ketchup, which ever goes with the rest of your meal.

Yield: 12 fritters

Soy
Isolate

6 medium potatoes, peeled and
  grated (3 cups)

1 medium onion, finely chopped
  or grated
⅔ cup soy protein isolate
2 tablespoons unbleached white
  flour
½ teaspoon salt
¼ teaspoon black pepper

1

Put the grated potatoes in a bowl of cold water while you prepare the onions. Drain the potatoes in a colander, and push out any extra water.

2

Place them in a bowl along with the other ingredients. At this point, you can use your hands to do the mixing. By squeezing the mixture with your fingers, you are able to work in all the ingredients.

3

When everything is mixed together, form 2-inch balls.

4

Heat a lightly oiled skillet to medium-hot. Place the balls on the skillet, and flatten them with a spatula. Cook for about 5 minutes on each side. The fritters will turn golden brown; watch them so they don't get too dark.

Per fritter: Calories 86, Total Protein 5 g, Soy Protein 4 g, Fat 0 g, Carbohydrates 16 g,
Calcium 14 mg, Fiber 2 g, Sodium 148 mg

Scalloped Potatoes

Yield: 6 servings

Soymilk

1

Preheat the oven to 350°F.

2

Oil a 9 x 13-inch pan and build layers. Start with a layer of the sliced potatoes, then sprinkle them with the chopped onions, flour, salt, and pepper. Dot the layer with margarine, and repeat.

3

For the top, spread a layer of potatoes and onions, sprinkle with salt and pepper, and dot with margarine.

4

Pour the soymilk slowly into the pan until it almost covers the top layer of potatoes. Cover with aluminum foil and bake for 30 minutes, then uncover and bake for 30 more minutes or until the potatoes are tender.

8 to 10 medium white potatoes, thinly sliced
1 to 2 onions, finely chopped
⅓ cup unbleached white flour
Salt and pepper
⅓ to ½ cup soy margarine

1 quart soymilk

Per serving: Calories 407, Total Protein 8 g, Soy Protein 4 g, Fat 14 g, Carbohydrates 62 g, Calcium 44 mg, Fiber 7 g, Sodium 166 mg

Tofu-Potato Souffle

Serve these savory, fluffy potatoes as a main dish or side dish.

Yield: 6 cups

Tofu

2 pounds russet potatoes
1 large onion, chopped
6 cloves garlic, minced
1 tablespoon olive oil
1 (12.3-ounce) package silken tofu
2 tablespoons chopped fresh
  parsley
1 teaspoon salt
¼ teaspoon freshly ground black
  pepper

1

Steam the potatoes until tender.

2

Sauté the onion and garlic in the olive oil until transparent.

3

Preheat the oven to 350°F. Process the peeled potatoes and tofu in a food processor, or beat until smooth. Fold in the rest of the ingredients, and transfer to an oiled 2-quart casserole dish or loaf pan. Bake for 30 to 40 minutes until heated through and browned on top.

Per cup: Calories 102, Total Protein 4 g, Soy Protein 3 g, Fat 4 g, Carbohydrates 13 g, Calcium 32 mg, Fiber 2 g, Sodium 377 mg

Desserts &

Drinks

Apple Crisp

Yield: 6 servings

Topping:
⅓ cup margarine
1 cup rolled oats
⅔ cup soy protein isolate
¼ cup wheat germ
⅔ cup brown sugar
½ teaspoon salt
1 teaspoon vanilla

8 cups chopped apples
Juice of 2 lemons (approximately
⅓ cup)
1 tablespoon cinnamon
1 teaspoon allspice
2 to 4 tablespoons unbleached
white flour
1 cup brown or white sugar or a
combination

1

Preheat the oven to 350°F.

2

For the topping, cut the margarine into the the oats, soy protein isolate, wheat germ, ⅔ cup brown sugar, salt, and vanilla with a fork, and mix well.

3

Place the apples in a deep dish, 9-inch casserole, or baking pan. Drizzle the lemon juice and sprinkle the cinnamon, allspice, flour, and sugar over them, and mix it all together.

4

Sprinkle the topping over the apples, and cover with aluminum foil. Bake for 20 minutes. Remove the foil and bake for 10 more minutes, or until the top is golden brown.

Per serving: Calories 475, Total Protein 13 g, Soy Protein 9 g, Fat 11 g, Carbohydrates 80 g, Calcium 55 mg, Fiber 5 g, Sodium 418 mg

Applesauce Spice Cake

Yield: 6 to 8 pieces

Soy
Isolate

1

Preheat the oven to 350°F.

2

In a medium mixing bowl, mix the oil with the sugars, molasses, apple-sauce, and ginger.

3

Sift the flour, soy protein isolate, cinnamon, salt, baking powder, and baking soda into the applesauce mixture. Stir the batter until all the dry ingredients are absorbed.

4

Add the dates and walnuts, if using, and mix well. Pour the batter into an oiled 9-inch cake pan, and bake for 35 minutes.

⅓ cup canola oil
½ cup brown sugar
¼ cup white sugar
1 tablespoon molasses
1½ cups unsweetened
applesauce
1 tablespoon grated gingerroot, or
½ teaspoon ginger

2 cups unbleached white flour
½ cup soy protein isolate
1 teaspoon cinnamon
½ teaspoon salt
1 teaspoon baking powder
1 teaspoon baking soda

½ cup chopped dates or raisins
½ cup chopped walnuts (optional)

Per piece: Calories 357, Total Protein 9 g, Soy Protein 6 g, Fat 10 g, Carbohydrates 57 g, Calcium 116 mg, Fiber 3 g, Sodium 416 mg

Chocolate Cake

Yield: 8 servings

Soymilk

⅓ cup canola oil
½ cup water
1 cup sour soymilk, or 1 cup
    fresh soymilk and 1 tablespoon
    vinegar
1 teaspoon vanilla
1 cup sugar

Dry Ingredients:
2 cups unbleached white flour
¾ cup cocoa
⅓ cup soy protein isolate
2 teaspoons baking soda
½ teaspoon salt

1
Preheat the oven to 350°F.

2
With a whisk, beat the oil, water, sour soymilk, vanilla, and sugar together until a smooth batter is formed.

3
Sift the dry ingredients into the liquid mixture, and whisk together well until all the lumps are gone. Pour into 2 greased 9-inch cake pans, and bake for 25 minutes.

Vanilla Frosting

You can make this frosting in a food processor; it couldn't be easier.

**Yield: 2 to 2¼ cups
(enough to frost a double layer cake)**

1 teaspoon vanilla
⅓ cup margarine
6 to 8 tablespoons soymilk
¾ cup soy protein isolate

4 to 5 cups confectioners' sugar

1
Mix all the ingredients well except the confectioner's sugar.

2
Add the sugar and mix well until you have reached a good spreading consistency.

Per serving (with frosting): Calories 337, Total Protein 10 g, Soy Protein 4 g, Fat 11 g, Carbohydrates 50 g, Calcium 72 mg, Fiber 6 g, Sodium 183 mg

Pineapple Upside-Down Cake

Yield: 16 pieces

1

Spread the ⅓ cup canola oil evenly over the bottom of a 9 x 13-inch baking pan. Sprinkle the brown sugar over to cover. Arrange the pineapple slices in one layer next to each other on top of the brown sugar. Set aside while you prepare the cake batter.

2

In a medium mixing bowl, combine the liquid, vanilla, oil, and sugar.

3

Preheat the oven to 375°F. Sift the flour, soy protein isolate, salt, baking powder, and baking soda into the liquid mixture, and beat well. When smooth, pour the cake batter evenly over the pineapple slices in the pan.

4

Bake for 25 to 30 minutes, or until the middle is thoroughly cooked. Insert a toothpick in the middle. If it comes out clean, the cake is done. Remove from the oven and let cool for 10 minutes.

5

Place a serving platter or tray on top of the cake. Holding the tray and the cake pan, flip them over so the bottom of the cake pan is on top. Put the platter or tray down on the counter, and gently lift the cake pan off the cake, leaving

⅓ cup canola oil or melted margarine
1 cup loosely packed brown sugar
1 (20-ounce) can sliced pineapple (Save the juice for the cake batter.)

1¾ cups liquid (A combination of pineapple juice from the canned pineapple slices and soymilk is good.)
1 teaspoon vanilla
½ cup canola oil
1 cup white sugar

2½ cups unbleached white flour
⅔ cup soy protein isolate
½ teaspoon salt
2 teaspoons baking powder
1 teaspoon baking soda

the pineapple on top. If any of the pineapple slices or topping stick to the cake pan, slide them off with a spatula, and place them back on the cake.

Per piece: Calories 292, Total Protein 6 g, Soy Protein 4 g, Fat 12 g, Carbohydrates 42 g, Calcium 69 mg, Fiber 1 g, Sodium 167 mg

Chocolate Tofu Ganache

This is a special treat to top almost any cake. Try it on Chocolate Cake (page 128).

Yield: about 2 cups

Tofu

1¼ cups firm silken tofu
3 tablespoons corn syrup
6 ounces (1 cup) semisweet or
   bittersweet chocolate, chopped

1

Blend the tofu and corn syrup until smooth and creamy.

2

Microwave 2 minutes, whip, and microwave 1 more minute. Whip in the chocolate chips, let them melt, then whip again until smooth and blended.

3

Let the mixture cool, then whip and spread over the cake. Chill until firm and serve.

Per ¼ cup: Calories 154, Total Protein 5 g, Soy Protein 3 g, Fat 10 g, Carbohydrates 11 g, Calcium 27 mg, Fiber 2 g, Sodium 25 mg

Cheesecake

Yield: one 8-inch cheesecake (8 servings)

1
Preheat the oven to 350°F.

2
Combine the cheesecake filling ingredients, and blend in a food processor or blender until smooth and creamy. If you're using a blender, you will have to process the filling mixture in two batches.

3
Pour the filling into the pie shell, and bake for about 45 minutes, or until cracks start to form around the edge of the filling.

Cheesecake Filling:
1 pound soft tofu, crumbled
½ cup brown sugar
⅓ cup liquid sweetener of your choice
¼ cup oil
2 tablespoons lemon juice
1 tablespoon unbleached white flour
1 teaspoon vanilla
Pinch of salt

1 (8-inch) unbaked graham cracker crust

Per serving: Calories 323, Total Protein 5 g, Soy Protein 4 g, Fat 18 g, Carbohydrates 36 g, Calcium 78 mg, Fiber 1 g, Sodium 201 mg

Banana Tofu Cream Pie

Yield: 8 to 10 slices

Tofu

Crust:
¾ cup whole wheat pastry flour
¾ cup finely chopped nuts
6 tablespoons soy margarine,
   melted
2 tablespoons honey

Filling:
2 cups crumbled regular tofu
3 ripe bananas
½ cup honey
½ cup soy margarine or butter,
   melted
1 tablespoon vanilla
1 tablespoon lemon juice

1

Preheat the oven to 400°F.

2

Combine the crust ingredients thoroughly, and press into a pie plate. Bake
for 8 to 10 minutes, then cool completely.

3

Combine the filling ingredients in a
blender or food processor until creamy
smooth. Pour into the cooled pie crust,
and chill for 2 or 3 hours.

Banana Tofu Pudding: For a pudding,
use only 3 tablespoons margarine.

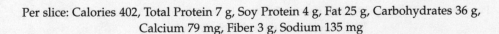

Per slice: Calories 402, Total Protein 7 g, Soy Protein 4 g, Fat 25 g, Carbohydrates 36 g,
Calcium 79 mg, Fiber 3 g, Sodium 135 mg

Creamy Chocolate Marble Pie

Yield: 1 (8-inch) pie (8 servings)

Tofu

1

Blend the tofu, sugar, oil, vanilla, and salt in a food processor or blender until smooth and creamy. Spread all but 1 cup of this mixture in the baked pie shell.

2

Add the cocoa to the 1 cup of pie filling left in the food processor. Process until the cocoa is mixed in, then drop by spoonfuls onto the pie. Draw a knife through the chocolate, swirling it through the vanilla mixture. Chill the pie until firm.

1 pound regular tofu
⅔ cup sugar
¼ cup oil
2 teaspoons vanilla
Pinch of salt

3 tablespoons cocoa

1 (8-inch) graham cracker crust, baked

Per serving: Calories 312, Total Protein 6 g, Soy Protein 4 g, Fat 18 g, Carbohydrates 32 g, Calcium 71 mg, Fiber 1 g, Sodium 198 mg

Creamy Coconut Pie

Quick and easy.

Yield: one 8-inch pie (8 to 10 servings)

Tofu

1½ pounds firm silken tofu
1½ cups confectioners' sugar
¼ cup oil
2 teaspoons vanilla
½ teaspoon salt
1 to 2 cups dried, sweetened coconut

1 (8-inch) graham cracker crust, baked

¼ cup dried, sweetened coconut

1

Preheat the oven to 350°F.

2

Blend the tofu, confectioners' sugar, oil, vanilla, and salt in a food processor or blender until smooth and creamy. Fold in the 1 to 2 cups dried coconut.

3

Pour into the pie shell, and bake for 15 minutes. Sprinkle on the ¼ cup coconut on top, and bake another 5 minutes or until the filling looks firm and set. Serve chilled.

Per serving: Calories 429, Total Protein 8 g, Soy Protein 5 g, Fat 29 g, Carbohydrates 29 g, Calcium 90 mg, Fiber 4 g, Sodium 37 mg

Fresh Blueberry Tofu Cream Pie

Substitute frozen blueberries if you can't find fresh ones.

Yield: one 9-inch pie (6 to 8 servings)

Tofu

1

Preheat the oven to 350°F.

2

To prepare the crust, process the flour and oil in a food processor until it is the consistency of cornmeal. While the processor is running, pour in the cold water. Process only long enough for the dough to start forming a ball. Gather the dough into a ball, and roll out to fit a 9-inch pie plate. Press into place if you need to.

3

To prepare the filling, blend the tofu, sweetener, flour, vanilla, and salt in a food processor or blender. Fold in the blueberries and pour into the unbaked 9-inch pastry shell. Bake for 45 minutes, cool, and serve.

Crust:
1 cup whole wheat pastry flour
2 tablespoons oil
¼ cup cold water

Filling:
1¼ cups silken tofu
½ cup fructose or sweetener of
  choice
¼ cup unbleached white flour
1 teaspoon vanilla
¼ teaspoon salt

3 cups fresh blueberries

Per serving: Calories 210, Total Protein 6 g, Soy Protein 3 g, Fat 4 g, Carbohydrates 36 g, Calcium 14 mg, Fiber 4 g, Sodium 121 mg

Key Lime Pie Filling

This filling can be used as pie filling or served as pudding or parfait. Since it is difficult to remove pesticides from citrus rind, try to use organic limes if available.

Yield: filling for one 9-inch pie (8 servings)

Soymilk

2½ cups soymilk
1 cup sweetener of choice
¾ cup fresh key lime juice
5 tablespoons cornstarch
2 teaspoons organic lime zest

1

Whip all the ingredients together until smooth.

2

Microwave Method: Pour in a 2-quart glass measuring cup or bowl, and cook on HIGH for 10 minutes, stopping to whip every 2 minutes.

3

Stovetop Method: Whip all the ingredients together in a saucepan, and heat over moderate heat, stirring constantly until thick and creamy.

4

Pour into a baked pie crust or serving dishes, and chill until firm. Top with Creamy Tofu Topping (page 137), and decorate with lime slices.

Per serving (filling only): Calories 139, Total Protein 2 g, Soy Protein 2 g, Fat 1 g, Carbohydrates 30 g, Calcium 5 mg, Fiber 1 g, Sodium 9 mg

Lemon Pie Filling

Yield: 8 servings

1

Combine the sugar, cornstarch, and salt in a saucepan, whisk in the soymilk and water, and bring to a boil over medium heat. Cook for 3 to 5 minutes, stirring often with a whisk. Remove from the heat.

2

Stir in the margarine, and slowly add the lemon juice and rind.

3

Pour into the crust, and chill. Before serving spread with Creamy Tofu Topping.

1½ cups sugar
½ cup plus 1 tablespoon cornstarch
¼ teaspoon salt
1¼ cups soymilk
1 cup water

3 tablespoons margarine
¾ cup lemon juice
Grated rind of 2 organic lemons

1 prepared graham cracker crust

Creamy Tofu Topping

This is an easy versatile, no-cholesterol topping you can use on a variety of desserts and treats.

Yield: 1½ cups

1

Combine all the ingredients in a blender or food processor until smooth and creamy.

1¼ cups firm silken tofu, crumbled
3 tablespoons sweetener of choice
1 teaspoon vanilla

Per serving (with topping): Calories 411, Total Protein 4 g, Soy Protein 3 g, Fat 14 g, Carbohydrates 66 g, Calcium 23 mg, Fiber 1 g, Sodium 315 mg

Lemon Tofu Cheesecake

This luscious treat has a creamy texture and a delicate flavor. It is easy to prepare. Try using fresh lime juice and zest for a variation in flavor. Use organic produce, if available, to avoid pesticides.

Yield: one 9-inch springform pan (8 to 12 servings)

Tofu

Crust:
1¼ cups graham cracker crumbs
(about 10 crackers)
2 tablespoons melted margarine
¼ cup granulated sweetener

Filling:
2½ cups firm silken tofu
6 tablespoons fresh lemon juice
½ cup sweetener of choice
2 teaspoons organic lemon zest
1 teaspoon vanilla

1

Preheat the oven to 350°F.

2

To prepare the crust, blend together the graham crackers, margarine, and sweetener in a blender or food processor. Pat into a 9-inch springform pan.

3

To prepare the filling, blend together the tofu, sweetener, lemon juice, lemon zest, and vanilla in a blender or food processor. Pour the filling into the prepared crust, and bake for about 45 minutes, or until small cracks start to form around the edges of the cheesecake.

Let cool, cut, and serve topped with fresh fruit, fruit filling, or Creamy Tofu Topping (page 137).

Per serving: Calories 161, Total Protein 5 g, Soy Protein 4 g, Fat 4 g, Carbohydrates 26 g, Calcium 1 mg, Fiber 0 g, Sodium 173 mg

Tofu Pumpkin Pie

Dairy-free, rich, creamy, and delicious.

Yield: one 9-inch pie (8 servings)

Tofu

1

Preheat the oven to 350° F.

2

Combine the filling ingredients in a blender or food processor until completely smooth. Pour into the pie crust, and bake for 1 hour, or until set.

3

Set aside to cool. Top with Creamy Tofu Topping (page 137), and serve.

Filling:
2 cups cooked pumpkin purée
¾ pound soft or firm silken tofu
½ cup honey
1 teaspoon cinnamon
1 teaspoon vanilla
½ teaspoon ginger
½ teaspoon nutmeg
¼ teaspoon salt

1 (9-inch) unbaked pie crust of your choice

Per serving: Calories 253, Total Protein 4 g, Soy Protein 3 g, Fat 9 g, Carbohydrates 36 g, Calcium 37 mg, Fiber 3 g, Sodium 262 mg

Strawberry Pudding or Pie Filling

Yield: 3½ cups

Tofu

1½ cups firm silken tofu
1½ cups fresh, ripe strawberries
½ cup sugar or sweetener of your
  choice
¼ cup oil
1 tablespoon lemon juice
1 teaspoon vanilla
Pinch of salt

1
Combine all the ingredient in a food processor or blender, and blend until smooth and creamy.

2
Pour into individual serving dishes or a baked pie shell, and chill overnight.

Per ½ cup: Calories 171, Total Protein 4 g, Soy Protein 4 g, Fat 10 g, Carbohydrates 16 g,
Calcium 60 mg, Fiber 1 g, Sodium 25 mg

Vanilla Pudding or Pie Filling

Yield: 6 servings

Soymilk

1

Combine the sugar, cornstarch, and salt in a medium saucepan. Gradually blend in the soymilk, stirring until smooth. Cover and cook over low heat, boiling gently for about 5 minutes.

2

Remove from the heat and blend in the margarine and vanilla. Pour into dessert cups or a baked pie crust, and chill. Top with Creamy Tofu Topping (page 137).

¾ cup sugar
¼ cup cornstarch
¼ teaspoon salt
3 cups soymilk

¼ cup margarine
2 teaspoons vanilla

Per serving: Calories 129, Total Protein 3 g, Soy Protein 3 g, Fat 1 g, Carbohydrates 8 g, Calcium 8 mg, Fiber 2 g, Sodium 193 mg

Coconut Date Bars

Yield: 25 to 30 bars

Soy
Yogurt

⅓ cup butter or margarine
1 cup brown sugar

1 teaspoon vanilla
¼ cup lemon juice
1 cup soy yogurt
1 cup dates, chopped
⅔ cup flaked coconut
1 cup rolled oats
½ cup soy protein isolate
1½ cups unbleached white flour
½ teaspoon salt
1 teaspoon baking powder
1 teaspoon baking soda

1

Preheat the oven to 350°F.

2

In a medium mixing bowl, mash the butter or margarine and brown sugar together with a fork. Add the remaining ingredients and mix well.

3

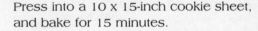

Press into a 10 x 15-inch cookie sheet, and bake for 15 minutes.

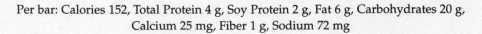

Per bar: Calories 152, Total Protein 4 g, Soy Protein 2 g, Fat 6 g, Carbohydrates 20 g,
Calcium 25 mg, Fiber 1 g, Sodium 72 mg

Molasses Cookies

A traditional treat with the added goodness of soy.

Yield: 28 to 30 cookies

Soy
Isolate

1

Preheat the oven to 350°F.

2

Combine the prunes and water in a blender, and blend until a thick paste is formed. Scrape into a medium mixing bowl, and add the rest of the wet ingredients. Stir together until a smooth mixture is formed.

3

Sift the dry ingredients into the bowl of liquid ingredients, and stir until completely mixed. Drop cookies by the tablespoon onto an ungreased cookie sheet, and flatten them with the bottom edge of the spoon. Bake for 8 to 10 minutes.

Wet Ingredients:
¼ cup dried prunes
3 tablespoons hot water

¼ cup canola oil
¼ cup blackstrap molasses
⅔ cup brown sugar
⅓ cup orange juice
1 teaspoon cider vinegar

Dry Ingredients:
2 cups unbleached white flour
⅔ cup soy protein isolate
1 teaspoon cinnamon
2 teaspoons ground ginger
¼ teaspoon ground cloves
1 teaspoon baking soda
½ teaspoon salt

Per cookie: Calories 162, Total Protein 5 g, Soy Protein 4 g, Fat g, Carbohydrates 26 g, Calcium 80 mg, Fiber 1 g, Sodium 132 mg

No-Bake Power Balls

These are a quick and easy kid-pleaser that are nutritious as well as delicious.

Yield: 42 to 46 balls

Soy Isolate

½ cup honey

½ cup peanut butter (medium consistency, not too oily or too dry)

½ teaspoon vanilla

½ cup chopped raisins

2 tablespoons roasted sesame seeds

1 cup soy protein isolate

¼ cup wheat germ, for rolling

1

Mix the honey, peanut butter, and vanilla together in a medium bowl until smooth. Add the raisins and sesame seeds, and mix again.

2

Carefully mix in the soy isolate until a smooth dough is formed. The mixture will be stiff yet sticky. With wet hands, grab a chunk of the mixture equal to about a heaping teaspoon, and roll it into a round ball, ¾ inch in diameter. (Keep a shallow bowl of water nearby to dip your hands in when you form the balls.)

3

Have a shallow bowl of wheat germ ready to roll the balls in. Make several balls, put them in the wheat germ bowl, and roll them around in the wheat germ until they are coated. Place them on a serving plate.

Per ball: Calories 93, Total Protein 6 g, Soy Protein 4 g, Fat 2 g, Carbohydrates 10 g, Calcium 16 mg, Fiber 1 g, Sodium 52 mg

Soft-Bake Chocolate Chip Cookies

An all-time favorite treat, now made more nutritious.

Yield: 24 cookies

1

Preheat the oven to 350°F.

2

In a medium mixing bowl, stir the oil, honey, sugar, vanilla, and soymilk together until a smooth batter is formed. Add the dry ingredients to the bowl, and stir well.

3

Add the chocolate chips and mix them into the cookie dough. Drop onto an ungreased cookie sheet by the tablespoon. These cookies can be placed 1 inch apart, they don't spread out as they bake.

4

Bake for 8 to 10 minutes. Watch carefully; they brown quickly.

Liquid Ingredients:
⅓ cup canola oil
⅓ cup honey
½ cup brown sugar
1 teaspoon vanilla
¼ cup soymilk

Dry Ingredients:
1 cup unbleached white flour
¾ cup soy protein isolate
½ cup rolled oats
1 teaspoon baking soda
½ teaspoon salt

¾ cup chocolate chips

Per cookie: Calories 112, Total Protein 4 g, Soy Protein 3 g, Fat 4 g, Carbohydrates 14 g, Calcium 16 mg, Fiber 1 g, Sodium 86 mg

Fruit Smoothie

A creamy and delicious pleaser!

Yield: 2 servings

Soy Isolate

1 cup chopped fresh peaches
1 cup soy yogurt
1 frozen banana
½ cup frozen blueberries
3 tablespoons soy protein isolate
½ teaspoon vanilla
Sugar to taste

1

Combine all the ingredients in a blender, and blend until smooth. Serve immediately.

Per serving: Calories 254, Total Protein 15 g, Soy Protein 14 g, Fat 4 g, Carbohydrates 34 g, Calcium 18 mg, Fiber 3 g, Sodium 137 mg

Vegan Eggnog

This "eggnog" will please even those who say they don't like soymilk. It's not too thick and cloying—a very refreshing drink any time of the year. Make the eggnog mix ahead of time, then blend with the ice cubes just before serving.

Yield: 10 servings

Tofu

1

Place the crumbled tofu and the soymilk in a blender with the sugar and salt. Blend until *very* smooth. Scrape this into a large bowl or pitcher, and whisk in the water, rum or brandy, and vanilla. Mix well, cover, and refrigerate until serving time.

2

To serve, blend half of the mixture in the blender with 10 of the ice cubes until frothy. Repeat with the other half. Serve in glasses with nutmeg sprinkled on top.

2 (12.3-ounce) packages soft silken tofu
2 cups soymilk
⅔ cup granulated sweetener of choice
½ teaspoon salt

1 cup cold water
1 cup rum or brandy or apple juice with rum or brandy flavoring to taste
4¼ teaspoons vanilla

20 ice cubes
Freshly grated nutmeg

Per cup: Calories 152, Total Protein 4 g, Soy Protein 4 g, Fat 3 g, Carbohydrates 15 g, Calcium 17 mg, Fiber 1 g, Sodium 63 mg

Cocoa or Carob Banana Soy Shake

This frothy shake makes a hearty snack.

Yield: 3 cups (2 servings)

1 cup soymilk
½ medium fresh or frozen banana
3 tablespoons sweetener of your
   choice, or to taste
1 tablespoon cocoa of carob
   powder

1

Combine all the ingredients in a blender, and blend until smooth and frothy.

Per serving: Calories 337, Total Protein 9 g, Soy Protein 7 g, Fat 5 g, Carbohydrates 63 g,
Calcium 27 mg, Fiber 8 g, Sodium 34 mg

Glossary

Amino acids: Chief components of a protein; the building blocks of living tissues. Eighteen different amino acids commonly occur in our food supply, and eight are considered essential because the body cannot produce them.

Antioxidant: Any naturally occurring or manufactured material whose incorporation into a fat provides a greater stability than that shown by the fat alone. The antioxidant increases stability by preventing or retarding reaction of the fat with oxygen, helping prevent rancidity. Antioxidants for food fats must be nontoxic and edible.

Defatted soy flour: Flour produced by removing most of the oil from soybeans with the use of hexane or other solvents. Defatted soy flour usually contains about 1% fat.

Extruder: A jacketed augur used to create the high pressures and temperatures needed to texturize soy flours or soy concentrates.

Full-fat soy flour: Ground whole soybeans containing all of the original oil, usually 18% to 20%. May be either enzyme active or toasted to minimize enzyme action. Also see "Soy flour."

Green vegetable soybeans: Vegetable-type soybeans picked green and cooked until tender. Used as a confection or snack. Sold in the pods, shelled, canned, or frozen. Called "edamame" in Japan.

High-fat soy flour: Soy flour produced by adding soy oil (with or without the addition of lecithin) to defatted soy flour to a desired level, usually in the range of 10 to 20%. Also see "Soy flour."

Hydrogenated vegetable oil: When vegetable oil is exposed to hydrogen gas in the presence of heat and a catalyst (nickel or copper chromite), the hydrogen combines with unsaturated fatty acids, resulting in an increase in the melting point of the oil; sometimes referred to as "hardening."

Hydrolyzed soy protein: A food additive made from soybean flours, concentrates, or isolates, treated with an acid or a base or an enzyme and then dried.

Isolated soy protein: Soy protein which has been removed and greatly concentrated from soybeans by chemical or mechanical means. It is generally produced by extracting protein from white soy flakes or soy flour with water or a mild alkali. Isolates usually have a protein content of at least 90%.

Koji: A Japanese term for the fungal starter culture used in soy sauce fermentation.

Lecithin: A fatty substance obtained from a variety of vegetable oils by the degumming process.

Low-fat soy flour: Flour produced either by partial removal of the oil from soybeans or by adding back soy oil and/or lecithin to defatted soy flour. Also see "Soy flour."

Meat analogs: Material usually prepared from vegetable protein to resemble specific meats in texture, color, and flavor.

Meat extenders: The use of soy or other vegetable proteins as partial substitutes for meat in processed items such as patties, chili, casseroles, etc.

Miso : A fermented, whitish-brown, brown, or red-brown seasoning paste made from soaked, steam-heated soybeans which are inoculated with cultures of microorganisms grown on rice or barley and then allowed to ferment. Typical microorganisms are Aspergillus oryzae, Aspergillus sojae, and Rhizopus oligosporus. One method of fermentation is called the "natural brewing process" in which the soybeans are allowed to ferment for approximately 9 months; the other method is known as "the quick brewing process" in which the miso is produced in a short time by reducing the length of time for processing (heating) the soybeans and the fermentation. Sweet and salty varieties are produced. Very popular in Japan, this product is know as "chiang" in China, "jang" in Korea, "tao-tsi" in the Philippines, and "tao-tjo" in Indonesia.

Natto: A whole soybean product produced in Japan by fermenting cooked soybeans with Bacillus natto until they develop a sticky, viscous coating. Also known as "tu-su" in China and "tao-si" in the Philippines.

Okara: Soybean pulp which remains after the production of soymilk. Okara consists primarily of the insoluble fiber of the soybean, along with some residual fat and protein. Also called "tou fu zha" in China.

Oxidation: A chemical reaction involving the addition or combination of oxygen with the other reacting material. Oxidation in fats or food products containing fat eventually results in development of rancidity and its accompanying objectionable flavors and odors. Hence oxidation of food fats is to be avoided.

Refining: Treatment of a natural or processed fat to remove impurities. Refining is accomplished by treatment of the fat with caustic soda, centrifuging, washing with water, and centrifuging again. The separated refined fat or oil is dried by heating under vacuum.

Solvent extracted: A product from which oil has been removed by solvents.

Soy Coffee: Coarsely ground, well roasted soy flour. Also known as "tadou kafei" in China

Soy flour: The finely powdered flour ground from dehulled soybeans after removal of most of the oil from by a mechanical or solvent extraction process.

Soy grits: The granular product ground from dehulled soybeans after removal of most of the oil by a mechanical or solvent extraction process.

Soy Nuggets: A group of salty, mold-fermented whole soybean products produced throughout East Asia. They are known as "hamanatto" in Japan, "touchi" in China, "tausi" in the Philippines, and "tauco" in Indonesia.

Soy protein concentrate: Prepared from dehulled soybean seeds by removing most of the fats. carbohydrates, and fiber. Soy protein concentrate must contain not less than 65% protein on a moisture-free basis.

Soy protein isolate: The protein portion of soybeans prepared by removing almost all of the fats, carbohydrates, and fiber from dehulled soybeans. Soy protein isolate must contain not less than 90% protein on a moisture-free basis.

Soy Sauce: A seasoning sauce of whole soybeans, soybean meal, or soy protein (sometimes mixed with wheat flour) which results from the action of molds, yeasts, and bacteria, as prepared by the Oriental method (with Aspergillus oryzae), or by being hydrolyzed with hydrochloric acid. With the Oriental method, the fermentation or enzymatic action is permitted to progress for up to one and a half years, at which time the extract is heated and processed to produce the liquid we know of as soy sauce. It is used as a seasoning in the preparation of foods, and as a table condiment. Soy sauce is known as "shoyu or tamari shoyu" in Japan and "lao chou, or "sheng chou" in China.

Soy Sprouts: Whole soybeans that have been sprouted (germinated) for up to six days. They are known as "taizu no moyashi" in Japan, "huangdouya" in China, and "kong na moal" in Korea.

Soybean curd: See Tofu

Soybean meal, mechanical extracted: The product obtained by grinding the cake or chips which remain after removal of most of the oil from soybeans by a mechanical extraction process. It must contain not more than 7% crude fiber.

Soybean meal: Ground soybean cake, ground soybean chips, or ground soybean flakes, sold according to its protein content, typically 44.0% High protein soybean meal contains: 47.5-49.0% protein.

Soybeans: A legume, the botanical name of which is Glycine max (L.) Merrill. The cultivated plant may reach a height of 3 feet or more. The seeds (soybeans) are borne in pods that grow in clusters of three to five, with each pod usually containing two or three or more seeds. The oil content of the soybean varies from 13% to 26% (average 18% to 22%) and from 38% to 45% protein (on a moisture-free basis). Soybeans were grown for centuries in the Orient and first introduced to the United States early in the 19th century. Soybeans grow best in areas having hot, damp summer weather but they can be grown under a great variety of climatic conditions. They are known as "taizu" in Japan and "tadou" in China.

Soyfoods: The term for edible soy-based products. These include traditional soyfoods such as tofu, soymilk, tempeh, soy sauce etc.; soy protein products produced after processing, such as soy flour, soy concentrates, and isolated soy proteins; soy oil products such as refined soy oil, hydrogenated soybean oil, and soybean lecithin; and, other edible by-products such as soybean hulls and soy fiber. Also, "second generation" soyfoods, a term to describe consumer-oriented products that use a soyfood as a primary ingredient, such as tofu, soymilk-based nondairy frozen desserts, or tofu-stuffed ravioli.

Soymilk: A protein-rich, milk-like liquid typically obtained from the soaking and grinding of whole soybeans with water (or hydrating whole, full-fat soy flour), cooking the resultant slurry, and filtering all or part of the soy pulp or fiber from the cooked liquid. Soymilk can be used to make tofu, spray-dried, or sweetened and flavored as a beverage. Soymilk is known as "tonyu " in Japan, " tou-chiang " in China, and "kong kook" in Korea.

Soynuts: Roasted whole soybeans. Sounuts can be oil-roasted or dry-roasted. They are also available plain, whole or crumbled, and flavored with sweetener or seasoning. Soynuts are known as "iri-mame" in Japan and "cui huangdou or chao tou" in China.

Tempeh: A soyfood product developed in Indonesia in which soybeans are soaked overnight and then cooked for a short time; the cooked soybeans are inoculated with the fungus Rhizopus oryzae and allowed to stand for 24 hours at 88°F (31°C) to permit optimum growth of the fungus sproes. The finished product resembles a pressed soybean cake. Tempeh should be steamed, fryed, or roasted before eating.

Textured soy concentrate: Soy protein concentrate that has been textured either by spinning it into a fiber and then combining the fiber in layers to achieve the desired texture or by a thermoplastic extrusion process.

Textured soy flour: Soy flour that has been textured imparted either by spinning it into a fiber and then combining the fiber in layers to achieve the desired texture or by a thermoplastic extrusion process. TVP® (textured vegetable protein) is a registered trademark of Archer Daniels Midland Company.

Textured soy protein: Soy protein that has been textured either by spinning it into a fiber and then combining the fiber in layers to achieve the desired texture or by a thermoplastic extrusion process.

Tofu (soybean curd): Formed (or formed and pressed) soymilk curds. Tofu is made when the protein in soymilk is coagulated with calcium sulfate, magnesium chloride (nigari), calcium chloride, or other coagulating agent and then placed into forming boxes (or a package as in "silken tofu"). Weight may or may not be applied to the tofu while being pressed to help in the removal of whey.

After solidification and cooling, the tofu is cut into pieces for packaging. Typically, tofu can have a protein content ranging from 5 to 15 percent. Tofu can be eaten as is or further processed by cooking or fermentation. Tofu can also be spray-dried to act as an ingredient in other food products, serving as a dairy or meat substitute. The name "tofu" is used in Japan, along with the term "kinugoshi." Tofu is also known as "toufu" in China and "doo bu" in Korea.

Yuba: Yuba is made by simmering soymilk at a near boil until a film forms, then lifting the film free and drying it. A popular product in Japan, it is also known as "doufu nao" in China.

U.S. & Canadian Soyfood Companies

21st Century Foods, Inc.
30A Germania St., Jamaica Plains, MA, 02130
  U.S.A.
PH: 617/522-7595; FAX: 617/522-8772
Products: soy cheese dairy analogs; soymilk beverages; tempeh; tofu & tofu products.

Agronico Inc.
Rural Route 1, P.O. Box 55, Le Center, MN, 56057
  U.S.A.
PH: 507/357-6027; FAX: 507/357-4242
Products: defatted soy flour; full fat soy flour; low fat soy flour; textured soy flour; soy oil; soymilk beverages; soymilk powder; textured vegetable protein; tofu powder.

Aloha Tofu Factory Inc.
961 Akepo Lane, Honolulu, HI, 96817 U.S.A.
PH: 808/845-2669; FAX: 808/848-4607
Products: tofu & tofu products.

American Food Company
4738 Valley Blvd., Los Angeles, CA, 90032 U.S.A.
PH: 213/223-7738; FAX: 213/223-8450
Products: soymilk beverages; tofu & tofu products.

American Hawaiian Soy Company
274 Kalihi St., Honolulu, HI, 96819 U.S.A.
PH: 808/841-8435
Products: miso.

American Health & Nutrition Inc.
508 Waymarket Drive, Ann Arbor, MI, 48103
  U.S.A.
PH: 313/994-7400; FAX: 313/994-4120
E-mail: ahn@organictrading.com
Internet: http://www.organictrading.com
Products: textured soy flour; soy oil; organic soybeans.

The American Miso Company
Affiliate of Great Eastern Sun, Inc.
Maple Creek Rd., Rutherfordton, NC, 28139 U.S.A.
PH: 704/287-2940; FAX: 704/286-0311
Products: miso.

American Natural Snacks
Affiliate of Tree of Life, Inc.
1755 Lakeside Drive, P.O. Box 1067, St. Augustine,
  FL, 32084 U.S.A.
PH: 904/825-2039; FAX: 904/825-2024
Products: soy cheese dairy analogs.

American Pride Soyfoods, Inc.
P. O. Box 524, Fairfield, IA, 52556 U.S.A.
PH: 515/ 472-4881
Products: tofu & tofu products.

American Soy Products
1474 North Woodland Dr., Saline, MI, 48176 U.S.A.
PH: 313/429-2310; FAX: 313/429-2112
Products: soymilk beverages.

Archer Daniels Midland Company
4666 Faries Parkway, P.O. Box 1470, Decatur, IL,
  62525 U.S.A.
PH: 217/424-5200; FAX: 217/424-5681
PH: 800/637-5850
Internet: http://www.admworld.com
Products: lecithin; meat analogs; defatted soy flour; enzyme-active soy flour; full fat soy flour; roasted soy flour; textured soy flour; soy grits; soy oil; soy oil margarine; soy oil shortening; soy protein concentrate; soy protein isolate; textured vegetable protein.

Arrowhead Mills, Inc.
110 S. Lawton, P.O. Box 2059, Hereford, TX, 79045
  U.S.A.
PH: 806/364-0730; FAX: 806/364-8242
Products: full fat soy flour; organic soybeans.

Ashland Soy Works
225 Water St., Ashland, OR, 97520-1883 U.S.A.
PH: 541/482-1865; FAX: 541/482-0744
E-mail: jmuhs@cdsnet.net
Products: soymilk beverages; tofu & tofu products; other soy-based foods.

Behm Seed Company
17730 30th Ave. NE, Atwater, MN, 56209-9511
  U.S.A.
PH: 320/974-3003; FAX: 320/974-3618
E-mail: behmm@aol.com
Products: organic soybeans; specialty soybeans.

Betsy's Tempeh
14780 Beardslee Road, Perry, MI, 48872 U.S.A.
PH: 517/675-5213
E-mail: pfaffg@pilot.msu.edu
Products: tempeh.

The Bridge
598 Washington Street, Midddletown, CT, 06457
U.S.A.
PH: 860/346-3663; FAX: 860/567-3304
Products: tofu & tofu products.

Cargill, Inc.
P.O. Box 5694, Minneapolis, MN, 55440 U.S.A.
PH: 612/742-5365; FAX: 612/742-5062
Products: defatted soy flour; low fat soy flour; soy
grits.

Cemac Foods Corporation
90 West Street, New York, NY, 10006 U.S.A.
PH: 212/964-9350; FAX: 212/791-1863
Products: soy cheese dairy analogs; other soy-
based foods.

Central Soya Company, Inc.
Protein Group
P.O. Box 1400, Fort Wayne, IN, 46801-1400 U.S.A.
PH: 219/425-5481; FAX: 219/425-5485
Products: full fat soy flour; soy protein concentrate;
textured vegetable protein.

Central Soyfoods
11 W. 14th Street, Lawrence, KS, 66044-3415 U.S.A.
PH: 913/843-0653
Products: soymilk beverages; tempeh; tofu & tofu
products.

Clarkson Grain Co., Inc.
Box 80, 320 East South St., Cerro Gordo, IL, 61818-
0080 U.S.A.
PH: 217/763-2861; FAX: 217/763-2111
Products: organic soybeans; specialty soybeans.

Clofine Dairy & Food Products, Inc.
1407 New Road, P.O. Box 335, Linwood, NJ, 08221
U.S.A.
PH: 609/653-1000; FAX: 609/653-0127
Products: soy fiber; full fat & low fat soy flour;
soymilk beverages; soymilk & tofu powder.

Cricklewood Soyfoods
250 Sally Ann Furnace Rd., Mertztown, PA, 19539
U.S.A.
PH: 610/682-4109
Products: meat analogs; tempeh.

Dae Han Tofu Company
737 S E Alder St., Portland, OR, 97214-2251 U.S.A.
PH: 503/233-8638; FAX: 503/233-8638
Products: tofu & tofu products.

Devansoy Farms, Inc.
202 W. 7th St., P.O. Box 885, Carroll, IA, 51401
U.S.A.
PH: 712/792-9665; FAX: 712/792-2712
E-mail: devansoy@pionet.net
Products: full fat soy flour; soy grits; soymilk bev-
erages; soymilk powder.

Eden Foods Inc.
701 Tecumseh Rd., Clinton, MI, 49236 U.S.A.
PH: 517/456-7424; FAX: 517/456-7025
Products: miso; soy sauce; soymilk beverages; tofu
& tofu products; organic soybeans; specialty soybeans.

Ener-G Foods, Inc.
5960 1st Ave. South, P.O. Box 84487, Seattle, WA,
98108-3248 U.S.A.
PH: 206/767-6660; PH: 800/331-5222; FAX:
206/764-3398
E-mail: heidi@ener-g.com
Internet: http://www.ener-g.com
Products: lecithin; meat analogs; soy fiber; full fat
soy flakes; defatted soy flour; enzyme-active soy
flour; full fat soy flour; low fat soy flour; roasted
soy flour; textured soy flour; soy grits; soymilk
beverages; soymilk powder; tofu powder.

Energy Sprouts & Texas Tofu
3602 High Point, San Antonio, TX, 78217 U.S.A.
PH: 210/654-3963; FAX: 210/654-3989
Products: tofu & tofu products; other soy-based
foods.

Farm Soy Company
96C The Farm, Summertown, TN, 38483 U.S.A.
PH: 931/964-2411; FAX: 931/964-2411
Products: soymilk yogurt dairy analog; soymilk
beverages; tempeh; tofu & tofu products; other
soy-based foods; organic soybeans.

Fearn Natural Foods
Affiliate of Modern Products, Inc.
3015 W. Vera Avenue, P.O. Box 09398, Milwaukee,
WI, 53209 U.S.A.
PH: 414/352-3333; FAX: 414/352-4478
Products: lecithin; meat analogs; full fat soy flour;
textured soy flour; soy grits; soy protein isolate.

Fresh Tofu Inc.
P.O. Box 1125, Easton, PA, 18044 U.S.A.
PH: 215/258-0883
Products: tofu & tofu products.

GeniSoy Products Co.
2300 South Watney Way, Suite D, Fairfield, CA,
94533
PH: 707/429-6147; 888/436-4769; FAX: 707/429-
6170
Products: isolated soy proteins; other soy-based
foods.

Great Eastern Sun, Inc.
92 McIntosh Road, Asheville, NC, 28806 U.S.A.
PH: 704/665-7790; FAX: 704/667-8051
E-mail: GESORGANIC@worldnet.att.net
Products: miso; soy sauce; other soy-based foods.

Hain Pure Foods Co.
50 Charles Lindbergh Blvd., Uniondale, NY, 11553
U.S.A.
PH: 516/237-6200
Products: soy cheese dairy analogs, soy-based ice
cream; tofu & tofu products.

Harvest Direct, Inc.
P.O. Box 988, Knoxville, TN, 37901-0988 U.S.A.
PH: 423/523-2304; FAX: 423/523-2304
E-mail: harvest@slip.net
Internet: http://www.midwest.net\creator\har-
vest
Products: meat analogs; soy fiber; textured soy
flour; soymilk beverages; soymilk powder; tofu &
tofu products.

Hawaiian Miso & Soy Company, Ltd.
1714 Mary Street, Honolulu, HI, 96819 U.S.A.
PH: 808/841-7354
Products: miso.

Health Valley Natural Foods, Inc.
16100 Foothill Blvd., Irwindale, CA, 91716 U.S.A.
PH: 818/334-3241; PH: 800/423-4846; FAX:
818/969-3687
Products: soymilk beverages.

House Foods America Corporation
7351 Orangewood Ave., Garden Grove, CA, 92841-
1411 U.S.A.
PH: 714/901-4350; FAX: 714/901-4235
E-mail: hinoichi@msn.com
Products: soymilk beverages; tofu & tofu products.

Houston Calco Inc.
2400 Dallas Street, Houston, TX, 77003 U.S.A.
PH: 713/236-8668; FAX: 713/236-1920
Products: soymilk beverages; tofu & tofu products.

Iowa Soy Specialties
6689 22nd Ave. Trail, Vinton, IA, 52349 U.S.A.
PH: 319/472-5656; FAX: 319/472-4568
E-mail: iasoyspec@www.mebbs.com
Products: full fat & low fat soy flour; soy grits; soy
oil; genetically modified & specialty soybeans.

Island Spring, Inc.
18846 103rd, S.W., P.O. Box 747, Vashon, WA, 98070
U.S.A.
PH: 206/463-9848; FAX: 206/463-5670
E-mail: lukoskie@walfenet.com
Products: meat analogs; soymilk beverages; tofu &
tofu products; other soy-based foods.

Kanai Tofu Factory
Affiliate of RMR, Inc.
515 Ward St., Honolulu, HI, 96814 U.S.A.
808/591-8205, 8225
Products: soy oil; tofu & tofu products.

Kapaa Poi Factory
1181 Kainahola Rd., Kapaa/Kauai, HI, 96746 U.S.A.
PH: 808/822-5426
Products: tofu & tofu products.

Kikkoman Foods, Inc.
Hwy. 14 & Six Corners Road, P.O. Box 69,
Walworth, WI, 53184 U.S.A.
PH: 414/275-6181; FAX: 414/275-9452
Products: soy sauce; other soy-based foods.

Kikkoman International, Inc.
50 California Street, Suite 3600, P.O. Box 420784,
  San Francisco, CA,
94142-0784 U.S.A.
PH: 415/956-7750; FAX: 415/956-7760
Products: soy sauce; tofu & tofu products.

LaChoy Food Products
901 Stryker St., Archbold, OH, 43502 U.S.A.
PH: 419-445-8015; FAX: 419-446-9278
Products: soy sauce.

La Soyarie Ltd.
94 Adrien Robert. St., Hull, Quebec, J8Y 3S2,
  CANADA
PH: 819/777-6716; FAX: 819/777-1093
Products: meat analogs; soynuts; tofu & tofu prod-
  ucts; other soy-based products.

Langeland Farms
3806 S. County Rd, 550 East, Greensburg, IN, 47240
  U.S.A.
PH: 812/663-9546; FAX: 812/662-6091
E-mail: grading@hsonline.net
Products: green vegetable soybeans; specialty soy-
  beans.

Lean Green Foods
P.O. Box 10562, Hilo, HI, 96721 U.S.A.
PH: 808/969-SOYB; FAX: 808/969-SOYB
E-mail: leangrn@interpac.net
Products: tempeh.

Lee Seed Company, Inc.
2242 IA 182, Inwood, IA, 51240 U.S.A.
PH: 712/753-4403; PH: 800/736-6530; FAX:
  712/753-4542
Products: soynuts, soynut butter; other soy-based
  foods; organic soybeans; specialty soybeans.

Lightlife Foods, Inc.
74 Fairview Street, P.O. Box 870, Greenfield, MA,
  01302 U.S.A.
PH: 413/774-6001; FAX: 413/772-2682
Products: meat analogs; tempeh; tofu & tofu products.

Living Farms
187 4th Street, P.O. Box 1127, Tracy, MN, 56175
  U.S.A.
PH: 507/629-4431; PH: 800/533-5320;
  FAX: 507/629-4253
Products: organic soybeans.

Lucas Meyer Inc.
Affiliate of Lucas Meyer GmbH & Co., Hamburg
P.O. Box 3218, Decatur, IL, 62524-3218 U.S.A.
PH: 217/875-3660; FAX: 217/877-5046
Products: lecithin; soy fiber; full fat soy flakes;
  defatted soy flour; full fat soy flour; low fat soy
  flour; textured soy flour; soy grits; soynuts.

Lumen Food Corporation
409 Scott Street, P. O. Box 350, Lake Charles, LA,
  70601 U.S.A.
PH: 318/436-6748; FAX: 318/436-1769
E-mail: lumenfoods@aol.com
Internet: http://www.lumenfds.com
Products: meat analogs.

The Mail Order Catalog
P.O. Box 180, Summertown, TN, 38483 U.S.A.
PH: 800/695-2241; FAX: 931/964-3518
E-mail: catalog@usit.net
Internet: http://www.healthy-eating.com
Products: meat analogs; soymilk powder; other
  soy-based foods.

Mandarin Soy Sauce, Inc.
4 Sands Station Rd., Middletown, NY, 10940 U.S.A.
PH: 914/343-1505; FAX: 914/343-0731
Products: soy sauce; other soy-based foods.

Michigan Soy Products
1213 North Main, Royal Oak, MI, 48067 U.S.A.
PH: 248/544-7742
Products: soymilk beverages; tofu & tofu products.

Mighty Soy, Inc.
1227 S. Eastern Ave., Los Angeles, CA, 90022
  U.S.A.
PH: 213/266-6969; FAX: 213/266-3844
Products: soymilk beverages; tofu & tofu products.

Mills Brothers International, Inc.
7066 S. 188th Street, Kent, WA, 98032 U.S.A.
PH: 206/575-3000; FAX: 206/251-0744
Products: specialty soybeans.

Miyako Oriental Foods, Inc.
Affiliate of Yamajirushi-Jyoza K.K., Japan
4287 Puente Avenue, Baldwin Park, CA, 91706
  U.S.A.
PH: 818/962-9633; FAX: 818/814-4569
Products: miso.

Morinaga Nutritional Foods Inc.
2050 W., 190 Street, Suite110, Torrance, CA, 90504
  U.S.A.
PH: 310/787-0200; FAX: 310/787-2727
E-mail: morinu@pakbell.net
Internet: http://www.morinu.com
Products: tofu & tofu products.

Nasoya Foods, Inc.
One New England Way, Ayer, MA, 01432 U.S.A.
PH: 978/772-6880; FAX: 978/772-6881
Internet: http://www.nasoya.com
Products: soymilk beverages; tofu & tofu products;
  other soy-based foods.

Natural, Inc.
6650 Santa Barbara Road, Elkridge, MD, 21227
  U.S.A.
PH: 410/796-3211; FAX: 410/796-3977
Products: meat alternatives; soymilk beverages;
  tofu & tofu products,

Natural Pacific Tofu
153 Makaala Street, P.O. Box 11001, Hilo, HI, 96721
  U.S.A.
PH: 808/934-0213
Products: soymilk beverages; tofu & tofu products.

Natural Products Inc.
798 Highway 6, Grinnell, IA, 50112-8004 U.S.A.
PH: 515/236-0852; FAX: 515/236-4835
E-mail: langsoy@avn.net
Products: enzyme-active soy flour; full fat soy
  flour; low fat soy flour; roasted soy flour; soy
  grits; soymilk powder; genetically modified soybeans; specialty soybeans.

Northern Soy
545 West Avenue, Rochester, NY, 14611 U.S.A.
PH: 716/235-8970; FAX: 716/235-3753
E-mail: soyboy@frontiernet.net
Products: meat analogs; tempeh; tofu & tofu prod-
  ucts.

Northland Soy Products
2905 Tanglewood Pl, Anchorage, AK, 99517 U.S.A.
PH: 907-248-2326
Products: tofu & tofu products.

Nutrisoya Foods, Inc.
4050 Pinard St., St. Hyacinth, Quebec J2S 8K4
  CANADA
PH: 514/796-4261; FAX: 514/796-1837
Products: soymilk beverages; tofu & tofu products.

Ota Tofu Company
812 S.E. Stark Street, Portland, OR, 97214 U.S.A.
PH: 503/232-8947
Products: tofu & tofu products; other soy-based
  foods.

Pacific Foods of Oregon, Inc.
19480 S.W. 97 Avenue, Tualatin, OR, 97062 U.S.A.
PH: 503/692-9666; FAX: 503/692-9610
Products: soymilk beverages; tofu & tofu products;
  other soy-based foods.

Pacific Soybean & Grain
One Sutter Street, Suite 300, San Francisco, CA,
  94104 U.S.A.
PH: 415/433-0867; FAX: 415/433-9494
Products: organic soybeans; specialty soybeans.

Panda Food Products, Inc.
1022 Pulaski Hwy, Goshen, NY, 10924 U.S.A.
PH: 914/651-4490; FAX: 914/651-4480
Products: tofu & tofu products; other soy-based
  foods.

PEDCO
270 7th Street, Wheeling, IL, 60090 U.S.A.
PH: 847/541-5513; FAX: 847/541-5513 *51
Products: soynuts.

Pillsbury Company
200 S. 6th Street, Minneapolis, MN, 55402 U.S.A.
PH: 612-330-4641; FAX: 612-330-4228
Products: meat analogs.

PMS Foods, Inc.
2701 E. 11th, P.O. Box 1099, Hutchinson, KS, 67504-
  1099 U.S.A.
PH: 316/663-5711; FAX: 316/663-7195
E-mail: sales@pmsfoods.com
Internet: http://www.pmsfoods.com
Products: meat analogs; textured soy flour.

Prosource, Inc.
601 Third Ave West, P.O. Box 1058, Alexandria,
MN, 56308 U.S.A.
PH: 320/763-2470; FAX: 320/763-7996
Products: green vegetable soybeans; dairy analogs;
meat analogs; soy fiber; soy protein concentrate;
hydrolyzed soy proteins; soy protein isolate;
soymilk beverages; soymilk powder; tofu & tofu
products; tofu powder; other soy-based foods;
organic soybeans; specialty soybeans.

Prosoya Foods Inc.
15350 56th Ave., Surrey, Vancouver, British
Columbia V4P 219 CANADA
PH: 604/532-8030; FAX: 604/576-6037
Products: soymilk beverages; other soy-based
foods.

Protein Technologies International, Inc.
Subsidiary of Ralston Purina Company
Checkerboard Square-13T, St. Louis, MO, 63164
U.S.A.
PH: 314/982-2736; PH: 800-325-7108;
FAX: 314/982-2461
Products: soy fiber; soy protein isolate.

Quong Hop & Company
161 Beacon Street, San Francisco, CA, 94080 U.S.A.
PH: 415/761-2022; FAX: 415/952-3329
Products: soymilk beverages; tempeh; tofu & tofu
products.

Rosewood Products Inc.
738 Airport Blvd., Suite #6, Ann Arbor, MI, 48108
U.S.A.
PH: 313/665-2222; FAX: 313/668-8430
Products: meat analogs; soymilk beverages; tem-
peh; tofu & tofu products.

Sacramento Tofu Company
8300 Belvedere Avenue, Sacramento, CA, 95826-
5902 U.S.A.
PH: 916/383-0725; FAX: 916/383-0725
Products: tofu & tofu products.

San-J International, Inc.
Affiliate of San-Jirushi Corp. Japan
2880 Sprouse Drive, Richmond, VA, 23231 U.S.A.
PH: 804/226-8333; FAX: 804/226-8383
E-mail: sanj@richmond.infi.net
Internet: http://www.infi.net/nsanj
Products: soy sauce.

Seymour Organic Foods
205 S. Main Street, P.O. Box 190, Seymour, IL,
61875 U.S.A.
PH: 217/687-4810; FAX: 312/687-4830
Products: lecithin; full fat soy flakes; full fat soy
flour; low fat soy flour; textured soy flour; soy
oil; soy protein isolate; soymilk beverages;
soymilk powder; organic soybeans.

Sharon's Finest
P.O. Box 5020, Santa Rosa, CA, 95402-5020 U.S.A.
PH: 707/576-7050; FAX: 707/545-7116
E-mail: richard@rella.com
Internet: http://www.rella.com
Products: soy cheese dairy analogs; meat analogs;
tempeh; tofu & tofu products.

The Simple Soyman
3901 N. 35th Street, P.O. Box 16677, Milwaukee,
WI, 53216-0677 U.S.A.
PH: 414/444-8638; FAX: 414/444-7519
E-mail: soyman@execpc.com
Products: meat analogs; tempeh; tofu & tofu prod-
ucts; other soy-based foods.

Smoke & Fire Natural Foods Inc.
P.O. Box 743, Great Barrington, MA, 01230-0743
U.S.A.
PH: 413/528-6891; FAX: 413/528-1877
E-mail: tofu@smokeandfire.com
Internet: http://www.smokeandfire.com
Products: tempeh; tofu & tofu products.

Sno Pac Foods, Inc.
379 S. Pine Street, Caledonia, MN, 55921 U.S.A.
PH: 507-724-5281; FAX: 507-724-5285
Products: organic soybeans, green vegetable soybeans.

Solnuts, Inc.
Affiliate of Solnuts, B.V.
711 7th Street, P.O. Box 450, Hudson, IA, 50643
U.S.A.
PH: 319/988-3221; FAX: 319/988-4647
Products: soy fiber; full fat soy flour; soy grits;
soynuts.

South River Miso Company
South River Farm, 888 Shelburne Falls Road,
 Conway, MA, 01341 U.S.A.
PH: 413/369-4057; FAX: 413/369-4299
E-mail: srmiso@javanet.com
Products: miso.

Sovex Natural Foods, Inc.
Affiliate of McKee Baking Company
9104 Apison Pike, P.O. Box 2178, Collegedale, TN,
 37315 U.S.A.
PH: 423/396-3145; PH: 800/227-2320; FAX:
 423/396-3402
Products: soymilk beverages; tofu & tofu products;
 other soy-based foods.

Soy City Foods
2847 Dundas St. W., Toronto, Ontario M6P 1Y6
 CANADA
PH: 416/762-3927; FAX: 416/762-1275
Products: meat analogs; tempeh; tofu & tofu prod-
 ucts; other soy-based foods.

Soyco Foods
Division of Galaxy Foods
2441 Viscount Row, Orlando, FL, 32809 U.S.A.
PH: 407/855-5500; PH: 800/441-9419; FAX:
 407/855-7485
E-mail: galxsales@galaxy foods.com
Internet: http://www.gqlaxyfoods.com
Products: soy cheese dairy analogs; meat analogs;
 soymilk beverages.

Soyfoods of America
1091 E. Hamilton Road, Duarte, CA, 91010 U.S.A.
PH: 818/358-3836; FAX: 818/358-4136
CONTACT: Ken Lee
Products: soymilk beverages; tofu & tofu products.

Spring Creek Natural Foods
212-C E. Main Street, Spencer, WV, 25276 U.S.A.
PH: 304/927-1815; FAX: 304/927-1815
Products: meat analogs; soymilk beverages; tofu &
 tofu products; other soy-based foods.

Springfield Creamery
29440 Airport Road, Eugene, OR, 97402-9524
 U.S.A.
PH: 503/689-2911; FAX: 503/689-2915
Products: soymilk yogurt dairy analog; other soy-
 based foods.

SunRich Inc.
#1 Elevator Avenue, P.O. Box 128, Hope, MN,
 56046 U.S.A.
PH: 507/451-3316; FAX: 507/451-2910
E-mail: sunrich@ll.net
Products: green vegetable soybeans; dairy analogs;
 soy fiber; enzyme-active soy flour; full fat soy
 flour; soy protein concentrate; soymilk beverages;
 soymilk powder; tofu & tofu products; tofu powder; organic soybeans; specialty soybeans.

Sunrise Soya Foods
729 Powell St., Vancouver, British Columbia V6A
 1H5 CANADA
PH: 604/245-8888; FAX: 604/251-1083
E-mail: sales@sunrise-soya.com
Internet: http://www.sunrise-soya.com
Products: soymilk beverages; tofu & tofu products.

Surata Soyfoods Co-op
325 West 3rd Ave., Bldg. A, Eugene, OR, 97401-
 2524 U.S.A.
PH: 541/485-6990; FAX: 541/345-0758
Products: tempeh; tofu & tofu products.

Sycamore Creek Company
Affiliate of Inari, Ltd.
200 State Street, Mason, MI, 48854 U.S.A.
PH: 517/676-3836; FAX: 517/676-6721
E-mail: stutz@msu.edu.com
Internet: http://designet.ml.org/sycamore
Products: soynuts; other soy-based foods.

Tacoma Tofu, Inc.
1302 Martin Luther King Jr. Way, Tacoma, WA,
 98405-3926 U.S.A.
PH: 206/627-5085; FAX: 206/627-1799
Products: soymilk beverages; tofu & tofu products.

Tofu Palace Products
P.O. Box 50085, Eugene, OR, 97405-0968 U.S.A.
PH: 541/683-4784; FAX: 541/683-4851
CONTACT: Toby Alves
Products: tofu & tofu products.

Tofu Shop Specialty Foods Inc.
100 Erickson Court, Suite 150, Arcata, CA, 95521
 U.S.A.
PH: 707/822-7401; FAX: 707/822-8982
Products: meat analogs; soymilk beverages; tofu &
 tofu products.

Tofutti Brands Inc.
50 Jackson Drive, Cranford, NJ, 07016 U.S.A.
PH: 908/272-2400; FAX: 908/272-9492
Products: soy cheese dairy analogs, soy-based ice cream; tofu & tofu products.

Tree of Life, Inc.
Affiliate of BolsWessanen, N.V.
1750 Tree Blvd., P.O. Box 410, St. Augustine, FL, 32085-0410 U.S.A.
PH: 904/825-2026; FAX: 904/825-2009
Internet: http://www.treeoflife.com
Products: soy grits; soy oil margarine; soy sauce; tofu & tofu products.

Turtle Island Foods, Inc.
P.O. Box 176, Hood River, OR, 97031 U.S.A.
PH: 541/386-7766; PH: 800/508-8100; FAX: 541/386-7754
E-mail: tifoods@aol.com
Internet: http://www.s/net.com/tif/tifhome.htm
Products: meat analogs; tempeh; tofu & tofu products; tofu powder.

Twin Oaks Community Foods
138 Twin Oaks Rd, Louisa, VA, 23093 U.S.A.
PH: 540/894-4112; FAX: 540/894-4112
E-mail: soyfoods@twinoaks.org
Internet: http://www.twinoaks.org/industry
Products: meat analogs; soymilk beverages; tempeh; tofu & tofu products.

Unisoya, Inc.
185 Voyer, St. Isidore Co., Laprairie, Quebec J0L 2A0 CANADA
PH: 514/454-5123; FAX: 514/454-5221
Products: meat analogs; tofu & tofu products; other soy-based foods.

Vitasoy USA Inc.
400 Oyster Point Blvd., Suite 201, South San Francisco, CA, 94080 U.S.A.
PH: 650/583-9888; FAX: 650/467-8910
Internet: http://www.vitasoy.com
Products: soymilk beverages; tofu & tofu products; other soy-based foods.

Westbrae Natural Foods
1065 E. Walnut St., Carson, CA, 90746 U.S.A.
PH: 310/886-8200; FAX: 310/886-8218
Products: miso; soy sauce; soymilk beverages.

White Wave, Inc.
1990 N. 57th Court, Boulder, CO, 80301 U.S.A.
PH: 303/443-3470; FAX: 303/443-3952
Products: soymilk yogurt dairy analog; meat analogs; soymilk beverages; tempeh; tofu & tofu products; other soy-based foods.

Wildwood Natural Foods
1560 Mansfield Avenue, Santa Cruz, CA, 95062 U.S.A.
PH: 408/476-4448; FAX: 408/479-3764
E-mail: iamemale@aol.com
Products: soymilk beverages; tempeh; tofu & tofu products.

Worthington Foods, Inc.
900 Proprietors Road, Worthington, OH, 43085 U.S.A.
PH: 614/885-9511; FAX: 614/885-2594
Products: meat analogs; soymilk beverages; textured vegetable protein; tofu & tofu products; other soy-based foods.

Wysong Corporation
1880 North Eastman, Midland, MI, 48640 U.S.A.
PH: 517/631-0009; FAX: 517/631-8801
E-mail: wysong@tm.net
Products: full fat soy flour; soy oil; other soy-based foods.

Yaupon Soyfoods
P.O. Box 672, Elgin, TX, 78621 U.S.A.
PH: 512/285-3810
Products: soymilk beverages; tempeh; tofu & tofu products.

Yves Veggie Cuisine
1638 Derwent Way, Delta, British Columbia V3M 6R9 CANADA
PH: 604/525-1345; FAX: 604/525-2555
E-mail: yvc@cyberstore.ca
Products: meat analogs; tofu & tofu products; other soy-based foods.

Sources of Information on Soyfoods:

Soyfoods Association of North America
1723 U Street, N.W.
Washington, DC 20009
Contact: Nancy Chapman, Exec. Director
PH: 202/986-5600
FAX: 202/387-5553
E-mail: info@soyfoods.org

Soyatech, Inc.
318 Main Street
P.O. Box 84
Bar Harbor, ME 04609
PH: 207/288-4969, 1/800/424-SOYA
Contact: Peter Golbitz, President
E-mail: data@soyatech.com
Internet: http://www.soyatech.com

United Soybean Board
c/o EvansGroup Public Relations
190 Queen Anne North
Seattle, WA 98109
PH: 206/285-5522, 1/800/TALK-SOY
FAX: 206/285-2551
Internet: http://www.talksoy.com

American Soybean Association
12125 Woodcrest Executive Drive
Suite 100
St. Louis, MO 63141
PH: 314/576-1770, 1/800/688-SOYA
FAX: 314/576-2786
Contact: Bob Callanan
E-mail: bcallanan@soy.org
Internet: http://www.oilseeds.org/asa/

Soyfoods Center
P.O. Box 234
Lafayette, Ca 94549-0234
Contact: William Shurtleff
PH: 510/283-2991
FAX: 510/283-9091

Nutrition Matters
1543 Lincoln St.
Port Townsend, WA 98368
PH: 360/379-9544
FAX: 360/379-9614
Contact: Mark Messina, Virginia Messina
E-mail: messina@olympus.net
Internet: http://www.olympus.net/messina/

An excellent book on soyfoods nutrition and
  health:
The Simple Soybean and Your Health
Mark Messina, PhD
Virginia Messina, RD
Published by Avery Publishing Group

Nutrient Content per 100 gram (3.5 ounce) serving

Composition & Nutrients	Moisture	Energy - Calories	Protein	Fats	Carbohydrates, by diff.	Fiber, total dietary	Ash	Calcium, Ca	Iron, Fe	Magnesium, Mg	Phosphorus, P
unit	g	kcal	g	g	g	g	g	mg	mg	mg	mg
Lecithin	0.0	763	0.0	100.0	0.0	0.0	0.0	0.0	0.0	0.0	0.0
Miso	41.5	206	11.8	6.1	28.0	5.4	12.7	66.0	2.7	42.0	153.0
Natto	55.0	212	17.7	11.0	14.4	5.4	1.9	217.0	8.6	115.0	174.0
Okara	81.6	77	3.2	1.7	12.5	4.1	0.9	80.0	1.3	26.0	60.0
Soy flour, defatted†	7.3	327	51.5	1.2	33.9	17.5	6.2	241.0	9.2	290.0	674.0
Soy flour, full-fat raw†	5.2	434	37.8	20.7	31.9	9.6	4.5	206.0	6.4	429.0	494.0
Soy flour, full-fat, roasted†	3.8	439	38.1	21.9	30.4	9.7	5.9	188.0	5.8	369.0	476.0
Soy flour, low-fat†	2.7	369	50.9	6.7	33.6	10.2	6.1	188.0	6.0	229.0	593.0
Soy protein concentrate, (alcohol extr.)†	5.8	328	63.6	0.5	25.4	3.8	4.7	363.0	10.8	315.0	839.0
Soy protein isolate, potassium type†	5.0	321	88.3	0.5	2.6	2.0	3.6	178.0	14.5	39.0	776.0
Soy protein isolate†	5.0	231	88.3	0.5	2.6	2.0	3.6	178.0	14.5	39.0	776.0
Soy sauce made from hydrolyzed veg. protein	75.7	41	2.4	0.1	7.7	0.5	14.1	5.0	1.5	6.0	93.0
Soy sauce made from soy (tamari)	66.0	60	10.5	0.1	5.6	0.8	17.8	20.0	2.4	40.0	130.0
Soy sauce made with wheat (shoyu) low sodium	71.1	53	5.2	0.1	8.5	0.8	15.2	17.0	2.0	34.0	110.0
Soybean oil, salad or cooking	0.0	884	0.0	100.0	0.0	0.0	0.0	0.0	0.0	0.0	0.3
Soybean oil, salad or cooking (hydrogenated)	0.0	884	0.0	100.0	0.0	0.0	0.0	0.0	0.0	0.0	0.0
Soybeans, green, raw	67.5	147	13.0	6.8	11.1	4.2	1.7	197.0	3.6	65.0	194.0
Soybeans, mature seeds, dry roasted	0.8	450	39.6	21.6	32.7	8.1	5.3	270.0	4.0	228.0	649.0
Soybeans, mature seeds, raw	8.5	416	36.5	19.9	30.2	9.3	4.9	277.0	15.7	280.0	704.0
Soybeans, mature seeds, roasted, no salt added	2.0	471	35.2	25.4	33.6	17.7	3.9	138.0	3.9	145.0	363.0
Soybeans, mature seeds, sprouted, raw	69.1	122	13.1	6.7	9.6	1.1	1.6	67.0	2.1	72.0	164.0
Soymilk concentrate (SANA Standards)*	≤86.0	n/a	≥6.0	≥2.0	n/a	n/a	n/a	n/a	n/a	n/a	n/a
Soymilk drink (SANA Standards)*	≤96.1	n/a	1.5-2.9	≥0.5	n/a	n/a	n/a	n/a	n/a	n/a	n/a
Soymilk powder (SANA Standards)*	≤10.0	n/a	≥38.0	≥13.0	n/a	n/a	n/a	n/a	n/a	n/a	n/a
Soymilk, (SANA Standards)*	≤93.0	n/a	≥3.0	≥1.0	n/a	n/a	n/a	n/a	n/a	n/a	n/a
Soymilk, fluid (as sampled by USDA)	93.3	33	2.8	1.9	1.8	1.3	0.3	4.0	0.6	19.0	49.0
Tempeh	55.0	199	19.0	7.7	17.0	3.0	1.4	93.0	2.3	70.0	206.0
Tofu, dried frozen (koyadofu)	5.8	480	47.9	30.3	14.6	7.2	1.4	364.0	9.7	59.0	483.0
Tofu, raw, firm	69.8	145	15.8	8.7	4.3	2.3	1.4	205.0	10.5	94.0	190.0
Tofu, raw, firm, prepared with calcium sulfate	69.8	145	15.8	8.7	4.3	2.3	1.4	683.0	10.5	58.0	190.0
Tofu, raw, regular	84.6	76	8.1	4.8	1.9	1.2	0.7	105.0	5.4	103.0	97.0

Explanations:
"n/a"= data not given
†Soy protein products calculated with a nitrogen factor of 6.25. All other soybean products calculated with a factor of 5.71.
*SANA Standards - Soyfoods Association of North America's voluntary industry standards for composition and labeling.

Sources: Composition of Foods, Raw, Processed, Prepared. Agriculture Handbook No. 8. United States Department of Agriculture (USDA), Consumer and Food Econ. Inst., Agricultural Research Service (ARS), Rev. Oct. 1975. Composition of Foods: Legume and Legume Products, Agricultural Handbook No. 8-16. USDA, Human Nutrition Service, Rev. Dec. 1996. USDA, ARS. 1996. USDA Nutrient Database for Standard Reference, Release 11. Nutrient Data Laboratory Home Page, http://www.nal.usda.gov/fnic/foodcomp.

Potassium, K	Sodium, Na	Zinc, Zn	Copper, Cu	Manganese, Mn	Vitamin C, ascorbic acid	Thiamine	Riboflavin	Niacin, nicotonic acid	Pantothenic acid	Vitamin B-6	Folate	Vitamin B-12	Vitamin A, IU	Vitamin A, RE	Vitamin E
mg	mg	mg	mg	mg	mg	mg	mg	mg	mg	mg	mcg	mcg	IU	RE	ATE
0.0	0.0	0.0	0.0	0.0	0.0	0.00	0.00	0.00	0.00	0.00	0.0	0.0	0	0.0	5.2
164.0	3,647.0	3.3	0.4	0.9	0.0	0.10	0.25	0.86	0.26	0.22	33.0	0.0	87	9.0	0.0
729.0	7.0	3.0	0.7	1.5	13.0	0.16	0.19	0.00	0.22	0.13	8.0	0.0	0	0.0	0.0
213.0	9.0	0.6	0.2	0.4	0.0	0.02	0.02	0.10	0.09	0.12	26.4	0.0	0	0.0	n/a
2,384.0	20.0	2.5	4.1	3.0	0.0	0.70	0.25	2.61	2.00	0.57	305.4	0.0	40	4.0	n/a
2,515.0	13.0	3.9	2.9	2.3	0.0	0.58	1.16	4.32	1.59	0.46	345.0	0.0	120	12.0	n/a
2,041.0	12.0	3.6	2.2	2.1	0.0	0.41	0.94	3.29	1.21	0.35	227.4	0.0	110	11.0	n/a
2,570.0	18.0	1.2	5.1	3.1	0.0	0.38	0.29	2.16	1.82	0.52	410.0	0.0	40	4.0	n/a
2,202.0	3.0	4.4	1.0	4.2	0.0	0.32	0.14	0.72	0.06	0.13	340.0	0.0	0	0.0	0.0
1,590.0	50.0	4.0	1.6	1.5	0.0	0.18	0.10	1.44	0.06	0.10	176.1	0.0	0	0.0	n/a
81.0	1,005.0	4.0	1.6	1.5	0.0	0.18	0.10	1.44	0.06	0.10	176.1	0.0	0	0.0	0.0
152.0	5,689.0	0.3	0.1	0.4	0.0	0.04	0.11	2.83	0.27	0.14	13.0	0.0	0	0.0	0.0
212.0	5,586.0	0.4	0.1	0.5	0.0	0.06	0.15	3.95	0.38	0.20	18.2	0.0	0	0.0	0.0
180.0	3,333.0	0.4	0.1	0.4	0.0	0.05	0.13	3.36	0.32	0.17	15.5	0.0	0	0.0	0.0
0.0	0.0	0.0	0.0	0.0	0.0	0.00	0.00	0.00	0.00	0.00	0.0	0.0	0	0.0	18.2
0.0	0.0	0.0	0.0	0.0	0.0	0.00	0.00	0.00	0.00	0.00	0.0	0.0	0	0.0	18.2
620.0	15.0	1.0	0.1	0.5	29.0	0.44	0.18	1.65	0.15	0.07	165.0	0.0	180	18.0	n/a
1,364.0	2.0	4.8	1.1	2.2	4.6	0.43	0.76	1.06	0.47	0.23	204.6	0.0	23	2.0	n/a
1,797.0	2.0	4.9	1.7	2.5	6.0	0.87	0.87	1.62	0.79	0.38	375.1	0.0	24	2.0	2.0
1,470.0	4.0	3.1	0.8	2.2	2.2	0.10	0.15	1.41	0.45	0.21	211.0	0.0	200	20.0	2.0
484.0	14.0	1.2	0.7	15.3	0.0	0.34	0.12	1.15	0.93	0.18	172.0	0.0	11	1.0	n/a
n/a	n/a	n/a	n/a	n/a	n/a	n/a	n/a	n/a	n/a	n/a	n/a	n/a	n/a	n/a	n/a
n/a	n/a	n/a	n/a	n/a	n/a	n/a	n/a	n/a	n/a	n/a	n/a	n/a	n/a	n/a	n/a
n/a	n/a	n/a	n/a	n/a	n/a	n/a	n/a	n/a	n/a	n/a	n/a	n/a	n/a	n/a	n/a
141.0	12.0	0.2	0.1	0.2	0.0	0.16	0.07	0.15	0.05	0.04	1.5	0.0	32	3.0	0.0
367.0	6.0	1.8	0.7	1.4	0.0	0.13	0.11	4.63	0.36	0.30	52.0	1.0	686	69.0	n/a
20.0	6.0	4.9	1.2	3.7	0.7	0.49	0.32	1.19	0.42	0.29	91.5	0.0	518	52.0	n/a
237.0	14.0	1.6	0.4	1.2	0.2	0.16	0.10	0.38	0.13	0.09	29.3	0.0	166	17.0	n/a
237.0	14.0	1.6	0.4	1.2	0.2	0.16	0.10	0.38	0.13	0.09	29.3	0.0	166	17.0	n/a
121.0	7.0	0.8	0.2	0.6	0.1	0.08	0.05	0.20	0.07	0.05	15.0	0.0	85	9.0	0.0

Nutrient Content per 100 gram (3.5 ounce) serving

Amino Acids

	Tryptophan	Threonine	Isoleucine	Leucine	Lysine	Methionine	Cystine	Phenylalanine
unit	g	g	g	g	g	g	g	g
Miso	0.14	0.64	0.81	1.13	0.66	0.15	0.10	0.60
Natto	0.22	0.81	0.93	1.51	1.15	0.21	0.22	0.94
Okara	0.05	0.13	0.16	0.24	0.21	0.04	0.04	0.16
Soy flour, defatted	0.68	2.04	2.28	3.83	3.13	0.63	0.76	2.45
Soy flour, full-fat raw	0.50	1.50	1.68	2.81	2.30	0.45	0.56	1.80
Soy flour, low-fat	0.68	2.02	2.26	3.79	3.10	0.63	0.75	2.43
Soy protein concentrate (alcohol extr.)	0.84	2.47	2.94	4.92	3.93	0.81	0.89	3.28
Soy protein isolate, potassium type	1.12	3.14	4.25	6.78	5.33	1.13	1.05	4.59
Soy sauce made from soy (Tamari)	0.18	0.41	0.49	0.74	0.73	0.17	0.11	0.53
Soy sauce made with wheat (Shoyu) low sodium	0.07	0.21	0.25	0.41	0.29	0.08	0.09	0.27
Soybeans, green, raw	0.16	0.52	0.57	0.93	0.78	0.16	0.12	0.59
Soybeans, mature seeds, raw	0.53	1.59	1.77	2.97	2.43	0.49	0.59	1.91
Soymilk, fluid	0.04	0.11	0.14	0.24	0.18	0.04	0.05	0.15
Tempeh	0.28	0.77	1.00	1.64	1.13	0.27	0.32	1.01
Tofu, raw, firm	0.25	0.64	0.78	1.12	1.04	0.20	0.22	0.77
Tofu, raw, regular	0.13	0.33	0.40	0.61	0.53	0.10	0.11	0.39

Fatty Acids

| | SATURATED FATS | | | | | | | | | | |
	TOTAL	6:0 caproic	8:0 caprylic	10:0 capric	12:0 lauric	14:0 myristic	16:0 palmitic	18:0 stearic	20:0 arachidic	22:0 behenic	24:0 tetracosanoic
unit	g	g	g	g	g	g	g	g	g	g	g
Lecithin	15.0	0.0	0.0	0.0	0.0	0.1	12.0	2.9	0.0	0.0	0.0
Soybean oil, salad or cooking	14.4	0.0	0.0	0.0	0.0	0.1	10.3	3.8	0.0	0.0	0.0
Soybean oil, salad or cooking (hydrogenated)	14.9	0.0	0.0	0.0	0.0	0.1	9.8	5.0	0.0	0.0	0.0

Sources: Composition of Foods, Raw, Processed, Prepared. Agriculture Handbook No. 8. United States Department of Agriculture (USDA), Consumer and Food Econ. Inst., Agricultural Research Service (ARS), Rev. Oct. 1975. Composition of Foods: Legume and Legume Products, Agricultural Handbook No. 8-16. USDA, Human Nutrition Service, Rev. Dec. 1996. USDA, ARS. 1996. USDA Nutrient Database for Standard Reference, Release 11. Nutrient Data Laboratory Home Page, http://www.nal.usda.gov/fnic/foodcomp.

Tyrosine	Valine	Arginine	Histidine	Alanine	Aspartic acid	Glutamic acid	Glycine	Proline	Serine
g	g	g	g	g	g	g	g	g	g
0.36	0.74	0.75	0.33	0.57	1.31	2.10	0.55	0.74	0.74
0.56	1.02	0.91	0.51	0.80	1.96	3.34	0.65	1.40	1.12
0.11	0.16	0.21	0.09	0.13	0.36	0.56	0.13	0.17	0.15
1.78	2.35	3.65	1.27	2.22	5.91	9.11	2.17	2.75	2.73
1.31	1.72	2.68	0.93	1.63	4.34	6.69	1.60	2.02	2.00
1.76	2.32	3.61	1.26	2.19	5.85	9.01	2.15	2.72	2.70
2.30	3.06	4.64	1.58	2.68	7.25	12.01	2.69	3.30	3.37
3.22	4.10	6.67	2.30	3.59	10.20	17.45	3.60	4.96	4.59
0.34	0.52	0.41	0.22	0.54	0.88	2.41	0.44	0.81	0.48
0.19	0.26	0.36	0.13	0.23	0.56	1.22	0.23	0.38	0.30
0.46	0.58	1.04	0.35	0.58	1.51	2.43	0.54	0.61	0.72
1.38	1.82	2.83	0.98	1.72	4.59	7.07	1.69	2.14	2.12
0.11	0.14	0.21	0.07	0.12	0.34	0.55	0.12	0.16	0.14
0.73	0.98	1.32	0.50	0.93	2.25	3.40	0.83	0.99	1.12
0.53	0.80	1.05	0.46	0.65	1.74	2.72	0.62	0.85	0.74
0.27	0.41	0.54	0.24	0.33	0.89	1.40	0.32	0.44	0.38

MONOSATURATED FATS					POLYUNSATURATED FATS								
TOTAL	16:1 palmitoleic	18:1 oleic	20:1 gadoleic	22:1 erucic	TOTAL	18:2 linoleic	18:3 linolenic	18:4 moroctic	20:4 arachidonic	20:5 timnodonic	22:5 clupanodonic	Cholesterol	Phytosterols
g	g	g	g	g	g	g	g	g	g	g	g	mg	mg
11.0	0.4	10.6	0.0	0.0	45.3	40.2	5.1	0.0	0.0	0.0	0.0	0.0	0.0
23.3	0.2	22.8	0.2	0.0	57.9	51.0	6.8	0.0	0.0	0.0	0.0	0.0	250.0
43.0	0.4	42.5	0.0	0.0	37.6	34.9	2.6	0.0	0.0	0.0	0.0	0.0	132.0

Recipes Indexed by Soyfood

General Index

Meet the recipe contributors to *Tofu & Soyfoods Cookery*–

Peter Golbitz
Peter Golbitz operated Island Tofu Works in Maine from 1980 to 1984. The recipe for "Tofurkey," a popular creation by Peter and his wife Sharyn Kingma, has appeared with many other of their tofu recipes in local newspapers.

Louise Hagler

Louise Hagler is an internationally renowned vegetarian chef, author, and soyfoods innovator. She is co-editor of *The New Farm Vegetarian Cookbook*, one of the first cookbooks to provide extensive instructions for making soyfoods at home and incorporating these foods in familiar recipes. Her book *Tofu Cookery*, first published in 1982, is the most popular tofu cookbook in America. Louise is also author of *Tofu Quick & Easy*, *Soyfoods Cookery*, and *Lighten Up! with Louise Hagler*.

Dorothy R. Bates

If you enjoy tempeh or textured soy protein, there's a good chance that your recipe collection includes something by Dorothy Bates. As the author of *The Tempeh Cookbook* and *The TVP®️ Cookbook*, Dorothy has made great contributions to our understanding of how to make delicious meals using soyfoods. She is also the author of *Kids Can Cook*, *Cooking with Gluten and Seitan*, co-editor of *The New Farm Vegetarian Cookbook*, and co-author of *Judy Brown's Guide to Natural Foods Cooking*.

Barb Bloomfield

Barb Bloomfield is an acclaimed cook from The Farm, America's largest vegetarian community, where she runs a vegetarian bed and breakfast. Barb is the author of *Soups On!* and *Fabulous Beans* and is the nutrition researcher for the Book Publishing Company's cookbook division.

Judy Brown

Judy Brown is widely known throughout the natural foods industry for her success in introducing soyfoods to the general public through tasting fairs, cooking classes, and natural foods demonstrations. She is the author of *The Natural Lunchbox*, co-author of *Judy Brown's Guide to Natural Foods Cooking*, and food editor for *Whole Foods* magazine.

Bryanna Clark Grogan

Bryanna has been a food writer for 30 years and is a frequent contributor to *Vegetarian Times* magazine. She specializes in low-fat vegan cooking and is author of *The Almost No-Fat Cookbook*, *The Almost No-Fat Holiday Cookbook*, *20 Minutes to Dinner*, and *Nonna's Italian Kitchen*.

Look for these vegetarian cookbooks
at your local bookstore
or order directly from Book Publishing Company.

Please add $2.50
shipping per book.

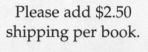

The Natural Lunchbox
$12.95

Fabulous Beans
$9.95

Tofu Cookery
$15.95

The Almost No Fat Cookbook
$12.95

Book Publishing Co.
P.O. Box 99
Summertown, TN
38483
800-695-2241

20 Minutes to Dinner
12.95

Look for these vegetarian cookbooks
at your local bookstore
or order directly from:

Book Publishing Co.
P.O. Box 99
Summertown, TN
38483
800-695-2241

Please add $2.50
shipping per book.

Soyfoods Cookery
$9.95

The TVP® Cookbook
$7.95

Tofu Quick & Easy
$8.95

The Tempeh Cookbook
$10.95